Practical Ansible

Configuration Management from Start to Finish

Second Edition

Vincent Sesto

Apress®

Practical Ansible: Configuration Management from Start to Finish

Vincent Sesto
Auckland, New Zealand

ISBN-13 (pbk): 978-1-4842-8642-5   ISBN-13 (electronic): 978-1-4842-8643-2
https://doi.org/10.1007/978-1-4842-8643-2

Copyright © 2022 by Vincent Sesto

Managing Director, Apress Media LLC: Welmoed Spahr
Acquisitions Editor: Aditee Mirashi
Development Editor: James Markham
Coordinating Editor: Aditee Mirashi

Cover designed by eStudioCalamar

Cover image designed by Freepik (www.freepik.com)

Distributed to the book trade worldwide by Springer Science+Business Media New York, 1 New York Plaza, Suite 4600, New York, NY 10004-1562, USA. Phone 1-800-SPRINGER, fax (201) 348-4505, e-mail orders-ny@springer-sbm.com, or visit www.springeronline.com. Apress Media, LLC is a California LLC and the sole member (owner) is Springer Science + Business Media Finance Inc (SSBM Finance Inc). SSBM Finance Inc is a **Delaware** corporation.

For information on translations, please e-mail booktranslations@springernature.com; for reprint, paperback, or audio rights, please e-mail bookpermissions@springernature.com.

Apress titles may be purchased in bulk for academic, corporate, or promotional use. eBook versions and licenses are also available for most titles. For more information, reference our Print and eBook Bulk Sales web page at http://www.apress.com/bulk-sales.

Any source code or other supplementary material referenced by the author in this book is available to readers on GitHub. For more detailed information, please visit http://www.apress.com/source-code.

Printed on acid-free paper

*This book is dedicated to Kirsty and our
two cats Rusty and Ash. Thanks for always
keeping me company while I'm writing and generally
helping me get the most out of life.*

Table of Contents

About the Author

Vincent Sesto is a DevOps engineer, endurance athlete, and author. As a DevOps engineer, he specializes working with Linux and open source applications. He is particularly interested in helping people get more from the tools they have and is currently developing his skills in DevOps, continuous integration, security, Splunk (UI and Reporting), and Python development.

About the Technical Reviewer

 **Lambodar Ray** is an IT professional in the United States. He is a database specialist with focused expertise in Amazon Cloud services and Oracle Cloud Infrastructure. He has worked in delivering database and infrastructure solutions in diverse industry and business domains including workforce management, finance, procurement, manufacturing, sales, and compensation. He is also a Certified Oracle Cloud Architect Professional and Amazon AWS Architect Associate.

Preface

In a world where we are constantly pushed to do more with less, configuration management has become a major cornerstone in allowing system administrators and DevOps engineers the ability to be more productive with the time they have. A configuration management tool which has been set up correctly and is keeping an environment patched and up to date will ensure that the ever-growing number of servers an administrator needs to work with will be as consistent as possible.

Combined with this, a configuration management system will also ensure changes that need to be made can be performed in an automated manner with ease. This is where Ansible comes in. This book hopes to bring you a unique approach to learning Ansible and configuration management while providing realistic examples in its day-to-day use.

This book is not aiming to provide you with 10,000 hours of courses for you to master the subjects outlined but instead provide you with necessary, deliberate training with a purpose in mind to give you a majority of the knowledge needed to be proficient at the subject at hand.

What This Book Covers

The book is divided into nine chapters which will allow you to build on your knowledge with each chapter, developing further as we move through the examples:

- **Chapter 1, Configuration Management with Ansible**, starts you off with the basics of Ansible, providing you details on how to install and configure your environment and how to get started working with different Ansible modules from the command line.

- **Chapter 2**, **Ansible Playbooks**, introduces you to the main way Ansible organizes tasks and code in playbooks. It is the perfect progression from the information you learned in the first chapter.

- **Chapter 3**, **Extending Playbooks with Roles and Templates**, provides you with the information you need to get you started with breaking down your configurations and organizing your code in roles.

- **Chapter 4**, **Custom Ansible Modules, Vaults, and Galaxies**, extends your knowledge on roles and playbooks by showing you how to start creating your own modules. It also shows you how you can keep secret data safe while getting you started with Ansible Galaxy.

- **Chapter 5**, **Working with Ansible in the Amazon Cloud**, will then show you how to get started working with Amazon Web Services (AWS) and allowing Ansible to do all the heavy lifting and hard work for you.

- **Chapter 6**, **Ansible Templates and CloudFormation Scripts**, will extend the work we did in the previous chapter allowing you to further enhance your roles to make them more reusable with Ansible template function. We will also start to incorporate AWS CloudFormation scripts into our deployment code.

- **Chapter 7**, **Ansible Troubleshooting and Variables**, will take you through how you can start checking your code before you deploy it to make sure you are limiting the number of errors during your configuration deployment.

- **Chapter 8, Testing Ansible with Molecule,** will introduce the Molecule testing framework into your configuration management allowing you to perform automated tests over your code and infrastructure.

- **Chapter 9, Managing Large Server Environments,** is the final chapter of the book and will discuss how you can work with a larger number of servers by manipulating your inventory files as well as introducing Ansible Tower to manage your Ansible code.

What You Need for This Book

To be able to work along with the example applications created in this book, you will need to have the following items available:

- A modern PC or laptop able to run up-to-date applications and virtualized servers.

- A running version of Ansible, preferably on Linux or Mac, but a majority of the commands will work across in Windows as well if you are using the Windows Subsystem for Linux.

- A modern and stable web browser, such as Chrome or Firefox.

- A basic understanding of web technologies as well as being competent using the Linux or Windows command line.

- Access to an Amazon Web Services account to deploy infrastructure to.

- An Internet connection.

Who This Book Is For

This book is designed to provide an in-depth introduction to Ansible and configuration management. It is best suited for system administrators, DevOps engineers, software engineers, and developers wanting to extend their current knowledge of computer systems and incorporate Ansible as a configuration management tool within them. This book is designed to provide an introduction to Ansible and allow the reader to build experience with each chapter to cover more advanced topics.

Conventions

In this book, you will find a number of text styles that distinguish between different kinds of information. Here are some examples of these styles and an explanation of their meaning.

A block of code is set as follows, with the number on the left representing the line number in the file. In most cases, the test will be highlighted in strong text to show that it needs to be added to your own code or file:

```
1 <xml>
2          <label>Value</label>
```

Any command-line input or output is written as follows where the command itself is in strong text and the output is listed below in the same font but in gray font color:

```
echo "Hello Ansible"
```

```
Hello Ansible
```

New terms and **important words** are shown in bold as these are texts you should be taking further note of.

Downloading the Example Code

You can download the example code files for this book from the following location: https://github.com/vincesesto/practical_ansible_ed2.

Piracy

Piracy of copyrighted material on the Internet is an ongoing problem across all media. If you come across any illegal copies of this book in any form on the Internet, please provide Apress with the location address or website name immediately at www.apress.com/gp/services/rights-permission/piracy.

Introduction

Technology is rapidly changing. In a short amount of time, we've seen technology become one of the most important parts of our world – from hardware like laptops and smartphones to social media and websites. Many people don't take the time to think of the underlying systems and infrastructure that a lot of this technology integrates with and in most cases relies on to work.

When the Internet was only starting to come to shape, a company could rely on one web server to provide all the information to their customers. Today, it's not uncommon for enterprise organizations to have hundreds or even thousands of servers to deliver reliable content to their customers. With this comes the complexity of making sure all these servers are consistent, secure, and up to date as well as being provisioned in a timely manner. This sounds daunting, but fortunately, technology and the way we administer and work with these complex systems have also changed.

This is where configuration management, and more so infrastructure as code, has allowed the people working with these systems to grow with their enterprises and ensure consistency and uptime. This is why Ansible has become one of the most popular tools to help teams and individuals manage and configure these systems. Ansible is an open source application that has been widely adopted and is also widely supported. This book hopes to show the reader why Ansible has been so widely adopted as its ease of use and functionality are helping companies across the world manage their systems. This book hopes to provide you with interesting and real-world projects to give you practical insight and hands-on experience that can then be transferred over to your own projects.

This book starts with a discussion on configuration management and introduces the reader to Ansible and some of the more common modules used in day-to-day work. The book then introduces the projects you will be working through and provides you with hands-on experience creating and working with Ansible playbooks, working with roles, and creating your own templates. The reader is then introduced to more advanced Ansible topics like creating your own Ansible modules, working with Ansible Galaxy, and storing your secrets and credentials with Ansible Vault.

The second half of the book then provides you with all you need to know to get started working with Ansible and provisioning infrastructure with Amazon Web Services. The book then finishes with the final chapter providing the reader with the tools they need to help troubleshoot their playbooks and roles as well as implementing testing for their infrastructure code.

Source Code

All source code used in this book can be found at github.com/apress/practical-ansible.

CHAPTER 1

Configuration Management with Ansible

Working with technology, we probably all started in a similar way. We created smaller computer systems, usually on the laptop or PC we were working on, or maybe a small, virtualized environment. As we developed our knowledge and experience, our systems grew larger and our need to keep all of these systems consistent grew with it.

Configuration management allows you to track items in your infrastructure and keep a track of what they do, what they're supposed to look like, and what's involved in creating them from the ground up. The type of information that this would include is the services they run, the **versions** of the applications being run, how they're configured, and their location in the network.

© Vincent Sesto 2022
V. Sesto, *Practical Ansible*, https://doi.org/10.1007/978-1-4842-8643-2_1

Our first chapter is going to get you started with Ansible as a means of managing the configuration of your environment. We're going to do our best to get you started as quickly as possible and try and limit the amount of text for you to read. In this chapter, we are going to cover the following:

- We will provide an introduction to **configuration management** and why it's so important.

- We will introduce **Ansible** and provide a brief discussion on why we have decided to use it as a configuration management solution.

- We will then get you started with **installation**, basic configuration, and running your first commands with Ansible.

- We will then go through some of the **common Ansible modules** to kick off your journey into configuration management.

An effective configuration management system can allow a software engineer or administrator the ability to view how to deploy and make changes to the working environment and even create the environment from scratch.

Getting Started with Configuration Management

An effective configuration management solution can benefit your environment in a number of ways including

- **Saving Time** – A configuration management system can help you reduce the time required to manage updates, changes, and repetitive tasks across multiple environments and networks.

- **Improving Availability** – Configuration management should help you resolve issues faster as it will allow you to identify, troubleshoot, and implement solutions to problems which could arise.

- **Lowering Your Risk** – It will help you reduce downtime and lower the chance of mistakes being made within the configuration of your services. It can also help you ensure your systems are secure and compliant.

- **Improve Control** – It will allow you to promote best practices across your environments and ensure consistency.

- **Allow You to Do More with Less** – This is probably the underlying reason for all these types of decisions. A good configuration management system will allow you to automate mundane processes and eventually allow you to spend less time worrying about your configuration management.

If you don't have an official way of managing your configurations, you most likely have developed a way to automate your deployment processes through scripts or a run book which would most likely start to become too complex to manage as your environments get bigger.

Why Ansible?

Ansible describes itself as software that automates software provisioning, configuration management, and application deployment. The first stable release of Ansible occurred in February 20, 2012, by Michael DeHaan. Ansible, Inc. was set up originally to commercially support and sponsor the application, with Red Hat acquiring it in October 2015.

Note   If you are interested in a more detailed history of how Ansible came about, Michael DeHaan has gone into great details in documenting the history of Ansible and its origins. Here is the link for his blog post on the origins of Ansible: `www.ansible.com/blog/2013/12/08/the-origins-of-ansible`.

If you haven't been working in technology for very long, you may not know there are a lot of ways in which you can implement configuration management. Some of the more popular open source projects include **Puppet**, **Chef**, **SaltStack**, and of course **Ansible**. There are benefits and reasons as to why you might choose one over the other. This book is focusing on Ansible due to the many benefits it provides including

- **Ansible Is Simple** – Ansible is easy to read, is minimal, and has a low learning curve to allow both administrators and developers to manage their environments with ease. Its configurations are human readable while being machine parsable, which will allow new team members to be onboarded quickly and existing team members the ability to make changes quicker. Although knowing Python and Linux shell scripting will help with creating your own modules, there is no need to know another scripting language to get the most out of the Ansible syntax.

- **Ansible Is State Driven** – Ansible will know how to get your system to that end state and will allow for reliable and repeatable IT infrastructure. Compared to a script, which is performing actions to get to the end state, this helps reduce the chance of the potential failure from occurring.

- **Ansible Is Secure** – As a default, Ansible uses SSH as its method of communication and its transport layer between servers and systems. It uses the open source version, **OpenSSH**, which is lightweight and available across many platforms. Being open source, it ensures that if a security issue is discovered, it will be patched by the community quickly. Ansible is also agentless, meaning you don't need to install another agent on your target machines.

- **Ansible Has Almost Everything Included** – Ansible is easy to deploy into new environments as it comes with almost everything included. When installed, Ansible comes with more than 1300 modules to get you started. If you can't find what you need in its preinstalled modules, Ansible Galaxy is an online community which allows you to reuse configuration code that were committed to the repository. If you are still stuck and if you know a little Python, you can even write your own module.

- **Simple Tasks Can Be Run from the Command Line** – You will see shortly in this chapter that we will be able to run commands on host machines without needing to create an Ansible playbook or other configuration file. You can simply run the command directly in the command line.

- **Ansible Is Idempotent** – If you get into a discussion with anyone about configuration management, sooner or later, the word idempotent will come up. Something is said to be idempotent if, whenever it is applied twice to any situation, it gives the same result as if it were applied once. Ansible is structured around the concept of being idempotent, meaning that you only do things that are required. Idempotent will also mean that nothing will be installed without needing to be, for example, if an application is already installed and up to date, it will not be installed again, if we run our Ansible command again.

Now that you have some more information on what Ansible is and why we are using it, the following section will guide you through getting started with installing and running your first Ansible commands.

Getting Started with Ansible

Let's not hold things up any longer. We will start by installing, configuring, and using Ansible. For now, we are simply going to install Ansible on the system we are working on.

We are going to focus on using Ansible with Linux, and all the commands we are going to be performing will be within a Linux environment. However, these commands should be able to work on a newer Windows installation, which has the Windows Subsystem for Linux installed as well as Ansible installed on a Mac. Originally, Ansible was designed to only work with Linux machines, but as of version 1.7, it also contains support for managing Windows machines.

Note   If you are running Windows and are interested in running the following Ansible commands, you can either install a virtual machine running a current version of Linux, you can install Docker containers and run the Ansible commands against the container, or you can install the Windows Subsystem for Linux. You may need to refer to the Windows documentation for your specific system, but the following commands should help you get there.

If you are running a newer version of Windows such as Windows 11 or the latest update of Windows 10, all you need to do to now install the Windows Subsystem for Linux is to open PowerShell and run the command **"wsl --install"**, but for older versions of Windows, you will need to run the following commands:

1. Open PowerShell as administrator and run the following command: dism.exe /online /enable-feature /featurename:Microsoft-Windows-Subsystem-Linux /all /norestart.

2. Once complete, restart your system when prompted.

3. When your system has restarted, go to the Windows Store and choose the Linux distribution that you are wanting to install. Preferably, choose Ubuntu as all the commands we are using should work without any issues.

4. Select "Get," and once the download has completed, select "Launch."

5. When the application starts up, it will load a console screen, and when the installation is complete, you will be prompted to create your UNIX user account for the Subsystem. The username and password will not have any relation to the current users set up on Windows.

6. If you haven't used the Subsystem before, compared to an actual Linux installation, it does run a little slower. Installation of applications may need some extra love to get going, but there is growing documentation and support as it is becoming a great way to work when you are only able to use a Windows environment.

Installing Ansible

Whether you are on Linux or Windows using the Linux Subsystem, you will be able to open up your Linux command line and run the following commands to install Ansible:

1. We should start by updating our package manager, so run the following apt-get update command using sudo to make sure you have privileged rights on your system:

   sudo apt-get update

2. Now we can install all the relevant dependencies which Ansible will rely on to install correctly using the following apt-get install command:

   sudo apt-get install python3 python3-pip git libffi-dev libssl-dev -y

3. Python's pip3 install command can now be used to install Ansible as we have here:

   pip3 install ansible
   ```
   Collecting ansible
     Downloading ansible-2.10.8.tar.gz (14.2 MB)
   |████████████████████████████████|
   |█████████████████| 14.2 MB 1.3 MB/s
   ...
   Installing collected packages: PyYAML, six, pycparser,
   cffi, cryptography, MarkupSafe, jinja2, ansible
   Successfully installed MarkupSafe-1.1.1 PyYAML-5.3.1
   ansible-2.10.8 cffi-1.14.0 cryptography-2.9.2
   jinja2-2.11.2 pycparser-2.20 six-1.15.0
   ```

We have redacted a lot of the output as pip3
installing Ansible also installs all the required
dependency packages needed for it to run
successfully. As well as Ansible, you'll see a number
of other applications installed as we have in the
preceding output.

4. Finally, to make sure that everything has worked
    correctly, we can now verify if Ansible has installed
    by using the ansible command with
    the --version option:

ansible --version
```
ansible 2.10.8
    config file = None
```
. . .

Ansible is now installed, and we have version 2.10.8
displayed from our output, but note that your
version may differ. I know, we're taking things a little
slow, but trust me, we will soon start to ramp things
up in the coming pages.

Note   As part of our installation, we have used the **pip3** command
to install Ansible in the previous steps. If you have not done this
before, the pip3 command is a tool for installing and managing
Python packages. Ansible is part of the Python Package Index, so pip3
is the perfect candidate for installing Ansible onto our system. If you
are having trouble installing this way, you may need to try running
the command as the root user. Also, if you are using a Mac, you can
simply use the same command to install Ansible on your system as
long as you have pip3 installed as well.

Ansible Support for SSH

Before we move on to perform our first Ansible command, we need to make sure **Secure Shell (SSH)** is working and operational on our system. As we've discussed earlier, Ansible uses **SSH** to communicate with other environments. Even though we will be running our first commands on the current system we are working on, we still need to make sure SSH is working and running successfully:

1. Make sure you are logged into your working environment, where you installed Ansible. First, we want to install **openssh-server** using the following apt-get install command:

    ```
    sudo apt-get install openssh-server -y
    ```

2. Once we have openssh installed, it will allow us to generate an ssh key to allow secure communication between servers. Using the **-t** option allows us to specify the type of key in this instance and **rsa** key:

    ```
    ssh-keygen -t rsa
    ```

3. Accept all the defaults and you will have your **id_rsa** private and public keys in the **.ssh** directory of your home directory.

4. If you perform a listing on the .ssh directory, you will be able to see the new keys generated. Your public key will have the **.pub** extension added to the end. Run the ls -l command as we have here from your home directory. The ownership of your files should be different to the following output:

    ```
    ls -l .ssh
    -rw---- 1 user user 1679 Jan 18 10:57 id_rsa
    -rw-r-r- 1 user user 398 Jan 18 10:57 id_rsa.pub
    ```

5. You can now copy the keys to your host. If you were going to send them to a different machine, you can simply substitute the domain or IP address for localhost in the following command. But for now, run the following command to copy your keys to your working environment:

`ssh-copy-id localhost`

6. This should now allow you to connect to your localhost via SSH, with the default openssh configurations allowing for the connection using the keys you generated previously:

`ssh localhost`

7. The preceding command will use the private key in your .ssh directory, which will be located in your home directory. If you need to refer to a key that is in a different location, use the -i option with ssh and specify the file name as part of the command:

`ssh -i your_ssh_key_file localhost`

You should now be able to perform a login into your environment without the need to input your username and password as SSH will use the newly created keys.

Note   If you are a fan of Docker or are familiar with how to work with Docker, there is also a Docker image available that has Ansible installed and ready to start accepting commands on. This is not the best way to use Docker as it does create a larger than usual image to be used, but it does give you an easy option to perform some of the exercises in this book. If you are interested in using this image instead of installing Ansible on your system, please go to the following URL as this will give you details on how to run and use the image:

```
https://hub.docker.com/repository/docker/
vincesestodocker/try-ansible
```

Finally, Our First Ansible Command

Now that we have Ansible installed and SSH configured, it's time to run our first Ansible command, so let's do this! From your console, run the following command:

`ansible all -i "localhost," -m shell -a 'echo Ansible is fun'`

```
localhost | CHANGED | rc=0 >>
Ansible is fun
```

It's a pretty basic command, but there is still a little to explain. The command does the following:

- Firstly, we specify **all**, so the command will be run across all the inventory we list.

- We then make a list of **inventory** with the **-i** option, but we only have our localhost listed, so this will be the only host the ansible command is run over.

- The **-m** option is then provided to allow us to specify a module we can use; in this case, it's the **shell** module to run a shell command.

- Finally, we specify the **-a** option, which allows us to provide arguments to the shell module, and in this instance, we are simply running an **echo** command to print the output "Ansible is fun".

If we wanted to run this command over multiple systems, we simply place a comma-separated list of the systems we want to run this Ansible command across as we have in the following command:

```
ansible all -i "localhost, 127.0.0.1" -m shell -a 'echo
Ansible is fun'

[WARNING]: A duplicate localhost-like entry was found
(127.0.0.1). First found localhost was localhost
localhost | CHANGED | rc=0 >>
Ansible is fun
127.0.0.1 | CHANGED | rc=0 >>
Ansible is fun
```

The preceding command has pointed to the same system by using "localhost, 127.0.0.1" as the list of systems we want to run our Ansible command over. We get a warning first as Ansible realizes that localhost and 127.0.0.1 are the same system, but then runs the command over both.

This is just the start of our configuration management journey. Imagine if you wanted to run this command across multiple servers, then you would only need to specify more hosts in the inventory. What if you didn't want to run an echo shell command? Well then, we could substitute a different command or use one of the many modules we will learn about later in this chapter. Finally, what if we wanted to do more than one simple command or deploy or change a whole environment? Then we would be able to run a playbook which includes all of these other commands.

Basic Ansible Playbooks

Playbooks are a way of using Ansible in a scripted form instead of running commands on the command line. We will quickly touch on the subject of playbooks now, but our next chapter will be dedicated to running you through all of the intricacies or working with playbooks. A playbook is a set of steps or tasks that need to be taken for a system to get to a certain end state. Let's not get too overloaded with details as we will go through this in our next chapter. So, for now, we can start by setting up a basic playbook and running it on our system to demonstrate how they work:

1. Make sure you are back in your development environment, and we want to start by creating a new file called **test.yml**:

    touch test.yml

2. Use your favorite text editor, open the file, and add the code listed as follows into the file:

```
1 ---
2 - hosts: localhost
3   tasks:
4     - name: Run our original Ansible command
5       debug: msg="Ansible is fun"
6     - name: We also need to test connectivity
7       ping:
```

The first line of the playbook let us know it's a **YAML** file with the three dashes (---), and the second line tells us we are only deploying to our **localhost**. From line 3, we then start a list of tasks which need to be run. The **name** directive in lines 4 and 6 provides a human-readable name and description for each of the tasks. Line 5 performs something similar to what we did in our first Ansible command providing output to the screen, and then finally, line 7 runs the **ping** module to test connectivity.

Note   Ansible uses YAML files as playbooks. This means that you really need to make sure your spaces and indentation are 100% consistent.

---

3.   To run your first playbook, we will use a new command. This time, we will use the following **ansible-playbook** command using the test.yml as our playbook and once again use the -i option as we did previously to specify the host we want to run our playbook on:

```
ansible-playbook test.yml -i "localhost,"

PLAY [localhost] *********************************

TASK [Gathering Facts] ***************************
ok: [localhost]

TASK [Run our original Ansible command] ***********
ok: [localhost] => {
    "msg": "Ansible is fun"
}
```

```
TASK [We also need to test connectivity] ***********
ok: [localhost]

PLAY RECAP *****************************************
localhost: ok=3 changed=0 unreachable=0 failed=0
skipped=0 rescued=0 ignored=0
```

Our output provides details of all the tasks being performed by the playbook, with the final line showing the system we are deploying to, the localhost, and three tasks performed in our playbook, with no changes, no unreachable hosts, and no failed tasks.

Ansible Configuration and Inventory Files

When you install Ansible, it will come with a long list of configurations that can be tweaked and tuned to your liking. As we saw in our previous examples, we have not done anything with our configuration file as the default configurations will be sufficient for the majority of the work you do.

If you have used Ansible before or have looked around, you will notice more than one location where configurations can be found. Ansible has precedence in using these configurations. It will use the first value found in the following order:

- **ANSIBLE_ENVIRONMENT_VARIABLES** – Usually specified in capital letters. Ansible will first look for variables defined as environment variables and use them before any other variables.

- **The ansible.cfg File** – This file needs to be located in the current directory where Ansible is being run from.

- **The .ansible.cfg File** – Usually specified in the user's home directory.

- **The /etc/ansible/ansible.cfg** – These are the system
  Ansible configurations created when the application is
  installed.

If you open the **/etc/ansible/ansible.cfg** with a text editor, you
will notice a majority, if not all, of the entries will be commented out.
When working in a different environment or system, keep the variable
precedence in mind. You may need to deploy a change from a different
environment where this system's Ansible variables may override what you
need to do. If you would like to get an explanation of any of the entries
in the configuration file, read through the Ansible documentation at the
following link:

```
https://docs.ansible.com/ansible/latest/installation_guide/
intro_configuration.html#explanation-of-values-by-section
```

As we saw in our previous example, we specified the details of our
systems within the command-line options. Instead, we can add an
inventory file that Ansible can refer to. This means we can add a lot more
detail to the inventory file with a long list of servers we want to manage. If
you are not already logged into your environment, do so, and we will set up
an inventory file to be used in our Ansible commands:

1. In the directory we are working in, we want to start
    by setting up an inventory of hosts we can run our
    commands on. We are going to call it "hosts," so
    create the file using the touch command as we
    have here:

    touch hosts

2. Open the hosts file with your favorite text editor
    ready to add our inventory details.

17

3. Our inventory file needs to group our hosts into different categories. For example, we may have a group called **[webserver]**, and underneath, we will list all of the hosts in our environment. For now, we are simply going to set up a category for the system we are working on as listed here:

```
1 [mylaptop]
2 localhost
```

As you can see, we have called the category "**mylaptop**" and placed it in square brackets. The domain or IP address is then placed below. If we have a second or third system which we wanted to include, we would simply add them below.

4. We can now run our Ansible commands by specifying the hosts file and no longer having to list the domain or IP addresses in our command. As you can see in the following command, we are still using the -i option, but now, we specify the hosts file:

```
ansible all -i hosts -m shell -a 'echo Ansible is fun'
```

```
localhost | CHANGED | rc=0 >>
Ansible is fun
```

This didn't look very impressive compared to what we've done previously. But remember we can now list multiple servers in our hosts file and refer to them by different names, or in our example, we can specify all to run the command across all the systems in our hosts file.

5. Open the hosts file again and add in a second value; this time, we will call it the [webserver] and list the IP address of our host again. The hosts file should now look similar to the following image:

```
1 [mylaptop]
2 localhost
3
4 [webserver]
5 127.0.0.1
```

6. For example, in the following command, instead of specifying all, it is just specifying webserver and will now only run the Ansible command over the host we have defined as a webserver:

ansible webserver -i hosts -m shell -a 'echo Ansible is fun'

```
localhost was localhost

127.0.0.1 | CHANGED | rc=0 >>

Ansible is fun
```

Hopefully, you can now start to see the benefit of using Ansible across your environment. In the next section, we are going to walk through some of the more common modules you might want to use in your configuration management.

Note   This may be a good time to remind you that as your configurations start to grow, it may be wise to consider placing your work under version control. As you may have read previously, all of the work in this book is provided to you via GitHub, and if you don't already use something similar, it is a perfect place to start managing your configurations and source code.

Running Ansible Modules

We discussed earlier in the chapter that Ansible comes with over 1300 modules as part of the installation. We've been using the "shell" module for our early attempts at running Ansible commands on our host. The shell module is simply a way for us to use Linux commands via Ansible. The modules available can be run directly on the remote hosts as we've been running our "shell" module, as well as being run through playbooks.

Ansible provides a handy index to all their modules. Due to the large number provided, the documentation has separated them into specific categories to help you search through for the specific ones you need. The full index of modules can be located at the following link:

```
http://docs.ansible.com/ansible/latest/modules_by_category.html
```

For the next few pages of this book, we're going to run through some common modules to help you get used to running Ansible commands and hopefully allow you to easily move on with creating playbooks in the next chapter. Log onto the system you've been working with so you can follow along.

Note   Even though the following pages are not specifically code, all of the commands are listed in the README file of the chapter_1 directory of this books code repository listed at the following location:`https://github.com/vincesesto/practical_ansible_ed2/blob/main/chapter_1/README.md`

Ping

One of the first modules a lot of people will learn is the **ping** module. As it suggests, and as we saw in our very first playbook, the module performs a ping test on the specified host requesting a reply if the host is accessible and powered on:

`ansible mylaptop -i hosts -m ping`

```
localhost | SUCCESS => {
    "ansible_facts": {
        "discovered_interpreter_python": "/usr/bin/python3"
    },
    "changed": false,
    "ping": "pong"
}
```

This is exactly the same as our previous commands we made earlier in the chapter where we have specified we want to run the module over **mylaptop** from the **hosts** inventory file. We then use the **-m** option to specify any module; in our case, we use the ping module. If all goes well, you will receive a **SUCCESS** reply.

Setup

The **setup** module provides us with over 1000 lines of information on our system, all of which are presented in a friendly-to-view **JSON** format, with all values being preceded with "**ansible_**" as you can see from the cut down output provided as follows. This command is useful to gather data on your system and then perform specific changes dependent on the information gathered. For example, a specific application will be installed depending on the specific type of operating system architecture being used by the system:

`ansible mylaptop -i hosts -m setup`

```
localhost | SUCCESS => {
    "ansible_facts": {
        "ansible_apparmor": {
            "status": "disabled"
        },
        "ansible_architecture": "x86_64",
        "ansible_bios_date": "03/14/2014",
        "ansible_bios_version": "1.00",
        "ansible_cmdline": {
        ...
        "ansible_userspace_architecture": "x86_64",
        "ansible_userspace_bits": "64",
        "ansible_virtualization_role": "guest",
        "ansible_virtualization_type": "docker",
        "discovered_interpreter_python": "/usr/bin/python3",
        "gather_subset": [
            "all"
        ],
```

```
        "module_setup": true
    },
    "changed": false
}
```

If you run the command on your system, you'll notice an output similar to the preceding one. In the last few lines of output, you will notice I am using a Docker image to run the commands, and as you can see, my ansible_virtualization_type is listed as docker.

Git

The git module allows you to perform **Git** commands via Ansible. If you need to deploy software directly from a git repository, this would be the perfect reason to use this module. You will need to have Git installed and available on your system before you are able to run the following command:

ansible mylaptop -i hosts -m git -a "repo='https://github. com/vincesesto/markdown-cheatsheet.git' dest=/tmp/markdown- cheatsheet/"

```
localhost | CHANGED => {
    "after": "ecfb900a44a84dcd0d798ad3b0c98ea838ea5668",
    "ansible_facts": {
        "discovered_interpreter_python": "/usr/bin/python3"
    },
    "before": null,
    "changed": true
}
```

In the preceding example, we have called the **git** module with the **-m** option and used the **-a** option to provide all the arguments specific to the module for it to successfully complete. In this case, we have specified the repository with **repo** argument and then provided a destination folder with the **dest** argument. If the folder is not present, Ansible will create it, so we should see the file downloaded and available in our destination folder. This Ansible command simply performs a **git clone** command. You would then need to perform the build process separately once the code is cloned.

Shell

We've used the **shell** module previously in this chapter, but in the following example, we have used it to verify our previous Git command worked by performing a listing of the files in the /tmp/ directory:

```
ansible mylaptop -i hosts -m shell -a "ls -l /tmp/"

localhost | CHANGED | rc=0 >>
total 8
drwx------ 2 root root 4096 Jun 24 14:35 ansible_command_
payload_mwym06gg
drwxr-xr-x 3 root root 4096 Jun 24 14:21 markdown-cheatsheet
```

All of this should be looking very familiar to you by now as we are simply specifying the arguments of a directory listing with the **-a** option.

Apt (or Yum)

A majority of modules will be able to be run across different versions of Linux, but one that may differ is the **package manager** which is being used on the specific system. The following command uses **apt** as the module, but of course for **Red Hat** or **Centos**, you would use the **yum** module with the name being equal to **httpd**:

```
ansible mylaptop -i hosts -m apt -a "name=apache2
state=present"
localhost | CHANGED => {
    "ansible_facts": {
        "discovered_interpreter_python": "/usr/bin/python3"
    },
    "cache_update_time": 1592964803,
    "cache_updated": false,
    "changed": true,
    ...
        "Processing triggers for systemd
        (245.4-4ubuntu3.1) ...",
        "Processing triggers for libc-bin (2.31-0ubuntu9) ..."
    ]
}
```

Once again, we have removed quite a few lines of the preceding output to help with our explanation. You will then see the arguments provided as name of the application we want to install and the state, which in the preceding example, the name of the package being installed is **apache2** and the state is **present**. If we wanted to remove the application, we would use the same command but change the state to **absent**.

Note   If you are not accessing your system as the root user, some Ansible modules like the **apt** module may need to use the **--become** option as part of your command. The option ensures Ansible becomes a user which can install programs on this system, such as the root user, and it then requests a password to allow the install to continue.

Package

Instead of using either of the Apt or Yum modules to install an application, we can also use the Package module. This means Ansible will simply use the package manager available on the system to install the application we want. In our following example, we have used apache2 again as the application we wish to install, and we have done this to demonstrate how Ansible is idempotent. In this example, Ansible knows what the desired state is, and because apache2 is already installed, we see the "changed: false" result in the returned command output:

```
ansible mylaptop -i hosts -m package -a "name=apache2
state=present"
    localhost | SUCCESS => {
        "ansible_facts": {
            "discovered_interpreter_python": "/usr/bin/python3"
        },
        "cache_update_time": 1649059827,
        "cache_updated": false,
        "changed": false
    }
```

Once again, we have removed quite a few lines of the preceding output to help with our explanation. A lot of users will still use either Apt or Yum instead of Package, as the Ansible code provides a run book to the commands being used to set up a specific environment. If you are running the same application installation across multiple different operating systems, then Package may be the best module to use.

Service

The service module can be used to perform a start, restart, or stop on services that are installed and running on your system. As we have Apache running on our current host, we can test this out by making sure Apache is started and the web service is running by using the following Ansible command:

```
ansible mylaptop -i hosts -m service -a "name=apache2
state=started"

localhost | CHANGED => {
    "ansible_facts": {
        "discovered_interpreter_python": "/usr/bin/python3"
    },
    "changed": true,
    "name": "apache2",
    "state": "started"
}
```

The argument used by the service is either **started**, **stopped**, or **restarted**. We have started this service and have a nice output showing the apache2 web service is in a started state.

Get_url

We can now test the **apt** and **service** modules we ran previously with the **get_url** module which grabs content from HTTP, HTTPS, or any other Internet protocols. As we should have a working Apache server running from the previous Ansible commands we ran, we can now download the default page running on **http://localhost**:

```
ansible mylaptop -i hosts -m get_url -a "url=http://localhost
dest=/tmp/"
```

```
localhost | CHANGED => {
    "ansible_facts": {
        "discovered_interpreter_python": "/usr/bin/python3"
    },
    "changed": true,
    "checksum_dest": null,
    "checksum_src": "07993837ce7f0273a65b20db8ee9b24823da7e1e",
    "dest": "/tmp/index.html",
    "elapsed": 0,
    "gid": 0,
    "group": "root",
    "md5sum": "3526531ccd6c6a1d2340574a305a18f8",
    "mode": "0644",
    "msg": "OK (10918 bytes)",
    "owner": "root",
    "size": 10918,
    "src": "/root/.ansible/tmp/ansible--
    tmp-1592968304.457506-3385-208885727085828/tmpu2f59a1j",
    "state": "file",
    "status_code": 200,
    "uid": 0,
    "url": "http://localhost"
}
```

Once again, we need to specify the destination as part of the
arguments, as the module needs somewhere to place the content it
downloads from the website URL in our command. The output of our
command shows a 200 value as a status_code to show we have a successful
result from our command.

File

If you are looking to create a directory or file on an environment, you don't need to look any further than the **file** module. It simply takes the path of the directory or file you want to create and the permissions needed:

```
ansible mylaptop -i hosts -m file -a "path=/tmp/another_test
owner=root group=root state=directory"
```

```
localhost | CHANGED => {
    "ansible_facts": {
        "discovered_interpreter_python": "/usr/bin/python3"
    },
    "changed": true,
    "gid": 0,
    "group": "root",
    "mode": "0755",
    "owner": "root",
    "path": "/tmp/another_test",
    "size": 4096,
    "state": "directory",
    "uid": 0
}
```

As you can see, the arguments we put in place are fairly straightforward. We need to make sure that we include the state of the file, in this case, a directory. We have also specified the owner and group the directory needs to be assigned to.

User

Setting up users is easy with this **user** module. We can control the state of the account on the system as being absent or present to determine if it is created or removed:

```
ansible mylaptop -i hosts -m user -a "name=jsmith comment='Jane Smith' state=present"
```

```
localhost | CHANGED => {
    "ansible_facts": {
        "discovered_interpreter_python": "/usr/bin/python3"
    },
    "changed": true,
    "comment": "Jane Smith",
    "create_home": true,
    "group": 1000,
    "home": "/home/jsmith",
    "name": "jsmith",
    "shell": "/bin/sh",
    "state": "present",
    "system": false,
    "uid": 1000
}
```

Our output from the Ansible command gives us clear details of the user account created, even though the user would not be accessible as it does not have a password set. We could also add the password as an argument to set this upon creation.

We can double-check the new account has been created by searching the **/etc/passwd** file on our host:

```
cat /etc/passwd | grep jsmith
```

```
jsmith:x:1002:1002:Jane Smith:/home/jsmith:
```

As you may know, creating users in a Linux system gives you a large number of options to configure. We can see from the output there are a large number of arguments configured besides the name, comment, and state arguments. The user will be created with the default values unless you specify these arguments in the Ansible command.

Find

The find module can be run to find different files and directories that are available on the host system. The find module allows you to specify a path, age of the file, and the type of file and even search for files of a specific size. This module can let you search for old files that may no longer be used or larger files that may be filling up your disk space. The following Ansible command is looking through the /var/log/ path of our system, looking for directories that are older than a week:

```
ansible mylaptop -i hosts -m find -a "path=/var/log/ age=1w
file_type=directory"
localhost | SUCCESS => {
    "ansible_facts": {
        "discovered_interpreter_python": "/usr/bin/python3"
    },
    "changed": false,
    "examined": 11,
    "files": [
        {
            "atime": 1592814330.422783,
            "ctime": 1592814330.331783,
            "dev": 112,
            "gid": 102,
            "gr_name": "systemd-journal",
```

```
            "inode": 3150926,
            ...
            "xusr": true
        }
    ],
    "matched": 1,
    "msg": ""
}
```

We're running these commands on a new virtual system, so we only
have one directory on the system that is older than a week. The output
provides a large amount of data on each file found, so we have again
reduced the amount of data on our output provided.

We are using a lot of modules to perform basic configuration tasks on
your systems, but these are just scraping the surface and not a limit to what
we can do with Ansible. You'll find there is a module for almost anything
you want to do in your environment, and if there isn't one created, you
can create it yourself. The modules in this section of the chapter have
been used to help you get used to running and using the commands on
your system.

We have done a lot of work running modules, but we are hoping
that by learning the basic module syntax, it will help you to transfer your
knowledge across to using playbooks a little easier.

Running Ansible on Different Servers

So far, we have run our Ansible commands on the same server we have
been working on. We can continue to do this, but in the long run and to
get the most out of Ansible, we need to start setting up remote servers to
deploy our changes on.

We have already created our ssh credentials, so we can copy them over to a server you have access to with the same command we used on our own server:

ssh-copy-id <remote_host_ip>

By performing the ssh-copy-id command, it will copy the public ssh key into the authorized_keys file located in the .ssh directory. This can also be performed manually if you prefer. You will need to access the home directory of the user you are accessing the host from and manually add the values to the authorized_keys file.

We can now ssh to this server without a password.

Although it is faster, it is less secure to be running commands without a password. To allow this for your user that is accessing the remote server, you will need to make changes to the **sudoers** file. You can do this by using the visudo command and then adding in the following line to the end of the file:

<username> ALL=(ALL) NOPASSWD: ALL

If the user you are using now has access to run as sudo on a remote server, you should be able to perform the following command without any errors or needing to enter any passwords:

ssh user@remote_host "sudo echo hello"

```
hello
```

Note   Making changes to the sudoers file can always cause major problems on your environment. If you wish to make changes to the sudoers file, make sure you use the **visudo** command as it will verify changes you are making to the file before saving them, and hopefully, make sure you don't stop access to your server.

Different Versions of Ansible

Throughout this book, we will be using the free and **open source version** of Ansible, trying our best to use ansible version 2.10. We will try our best to ensure all scripts and code will be compatible with this version and any subsequent versions. A large majority of companies are using the open source version of Ansible as it gives them more than enough features to run a configuration management system suitable for even the largest of enterprises.

Ansible Tower is a paid version that is supported by Red Hat, but has a free basic license available for ten nodes. This is the enterprise version of Ansible which provides some extra bells and whistles that you don't get with the open source version of Ansible. It allows you to run ansible playbook projects, run playbooks, schedule playbooks, handle inventories of servers, and have a full access control list for managing users. It also has support provided to the end user along with a user-friendly dashboard.

Ansible Projects

We are just going to take a few moments to introduce the projects you will be working on over the remainder of the book. It's hoped these projects will provide you with real-world examples which build on each other as the chapters and your knowledge progress.

Basic LAMP Stack

As you may know, a **LAMP** stack stands for Linux, Apache, MySQL, PHP (or Python in our case) and is used to host web applications. In the first four chapters of this book, we are going to work through our first project. We will be set up a basic LAMP stack which will be configured to serve basic web content.

To take this a little further and to show you how we can take our Ansible configuration management further, we will expand this example to also use a **Django**-based server. If you haven't used Django before, it is a Python-based web framework, and although it can be used to create complex environments, we will only be using the basics of the application, so there will not be anything overwhelming or complicated in our example.

Splunk Server Environment

From Chapter 5, we are then going to move onto a different project where we will be setting up and configuring a Splunk server environment. Nothing is too exciting about this, but we will be moving our work into the Amazon Cloud. This project will take you through using Ansible in conjunction with using **Amazon Web Services**. We will start with the basics of setting up our instance, configuring and setting up instance user data, and then create an AWS image from our Splunk server.

From here, we will move further on and learn how to deploy our images into a server environment using both **Ansible** and **CloudFormation**. We will also use our image to pull in application code to be deployed when the server is started up. We will cover a lot of AWS work, but there will not be anything too intense and complicated as the main focus of our work will be Ansible.

Even though it is not large enough to note as a specific project, in Chapter 9, we will be working with Ansible Tower; more specifically, we will be using the free open source version called Ansible AWX. The chapter will show you how to install the application onto your environment. It is a little complex but comes with a handy Ansible playbook that will do a lot of the work for us.

Summary

We have started slow covering a lot of work on the basic aspects of Ansible, but you've still come a long way. At the start of the chapter, we began with a discussion on configuration management and how Ansible fits in with this. We then started to walk you through the process of installing, configuring, and running Ansible commands and then set up a basic Ansible playbook for you to run.

We then moved further into the configuration of Ansible for your environment and then onto the remainder of the chapter where we took you through some of the different versions of Ansible as well as the different types of modules available to you.

The next chapter will take you further into configuring and working with Ansible by introducing playbooks, and we will also get started with working on creating our LAMP stack which we will be developing further through the following chapters.

CHAPTER 2

Ansible Playbooks

I'm hoping by now you can see Ansible is an easy way to control applications and system configurations remotely. But running each command in the command line is not the most efficient way of deploying these changes to our environments. This is where we can introduce **playbooks**. Ansible playbooks can contain a play or multiple plays and help you automate system configurations. It has a reusable set of tasks that will step through the implementation of your system into its desired state.

In this chapter, we're going to introduce playbooks into your configuration management arsenal, helping you deploy your systems a lot easier. In this chapter

- We start by taking a look at **YAML syntax** and how we use it in our playbooks.

- We then move on to converting some of the command-line modules we learned in our last chapter into an Ansible playbook which will be the start of our **LAMP stack project**.

- Our focus then moves to the specifics of our working playbooks and how they function.

- We will then take our project further by creating a **database** and integrating **Python** in our environments all by using playbooks.

© Vincent Sesto 2022
V. Sesto, *Practical Ansible*, https://doi.org/10.1007/978-1-4842-8643-2_2

- We finally take a look at how we can make our
  playbooks more **reusable** especially when things get
  more complex using the import and include functions.

In our last chapter, we mentioned that each playbook includes a set of plays, which map a group of hosts to a specific role. In the following example, a host will be mapped to a web server role. A list of tasks represents the roles. These specific tasks act as a recipe, using our Ansible modules to deploy our system to one particular state. Before we start to work more on our playbooks, we will first understand how YAML syntax works, so we can be more proficient in implementing our playbooks later in the chapter.

Ansible and YAML Syntax

Before we move into using playbooks in Ansible, we need to take a quick moment to discuss **YAML** syntax. As we discussed in the first chapter of this book, our basic Ansible playbook used YAML syntax to output a simple message to the screen. The goal of YAML is to be easily readable by humans. If you've used similar configuration file formats like **XML** or **JSON**, you will notice YAML is also a lot easier to read compared to these other formats.

With YAML being the basis of our Ansible playbooks, it's appropriate to run through the basics of the syntax before moving on to more playbook examples. If you're already familiar with working with YAML, feel free to move ahead to the next section of the chapter:

- **YAML File Names End with .yml** – All our playbooks
  will use the .yml or .yaml file name extension, and this
  lets everyone know it's a YAML format file.

- **Syntax Starts with Three Dashes** – The first thing you'll notice is our plays in playbooks all start with three dashes (---). This will allow applications reading the file to know it is a YAML format file.

- **Whitespace Denotes Structure** – Indentation and **whitespace** in our YAML file denote the structure of the file. If your indentation is out of place, this could mean your configuration or playbooks are not being read correctly. Make sure you never use a tab character as an indentation.

- **A Comment Uses the Hash Symbol** – You'll most likely want to use comments through your playbook. All comments are preceded with the **hash (#)** symbol.

- **List Members Use a Leading Hyphen** – When displaying a list of items, all items in the list will begin at the same indentation level and start with a **hyphen (-)**. Here is an example list of operating systems, using two spaces and then a hyphen before each of the values:

```
---
Operating Systems:
  - Ubuntu
  - Debian
  - Red Hat
  - Centos
  - Windows
  - Mac
```

- **Dictionaries Are Represented As a "Key: Value"** – We simply add values to a dictionary by indenting our values after the dictionary name and then adding a key-value pair on each line. Here is an example of a dictionary in YAML where we have two dictionaries, one named vince and the second named neil. Both then have three key-value pairs added in each with keys specified as full_name, job, and comment:

```
---
vince:
  full_name: Vincent Sesto
  job: devops engineer
  comment: Ansible is Fun!
neil:
  full_name: Neil Diamond
  job: Singer and Songwriter
  comment: Good Lord!
```

- **Span Multiple Lines with a Pipe** – When needing to add multiple lines of data for one entry, you can use the **pipe (|)** symbol to add multiple lines and will include the new line in the YAML file, while using the **less than (>)** symbol will ignore any new lines. In the following example, we are setting environment variables to be used on a system and are using the pipe symbol to have all new line characters present:

```
env: |-
  DB_HOST= "database.host.com"
  DB_DATABASE= "testdb"
  DB_USERNAME= "dbadmin"
  SUDO= "root"
  JAVA_HOME= "/usr/lib/jvm/java-11-oracle"
  HOME= "/home/ubuntu"
  USER= "ubuntu"
  MAIL= "/var/mail/ubuntu"
```

The following example is using the less than symbol
to create a message of the day entry where the
following four lines will all be listed on one line:

```
motd: >
  Welcome to your new system
  where everything from this
  message should be on the
  same line.
```

YAML is an acronym for **"YAML Ain't Markup Language"** or "Yet
Another Markup Language" and is being widely used across different
languages due to the ease of reading and the fact it is being widely
supported by different programming languages. We have only touched on
the basics of YAML, and this should be enough for you to continue with the
next chapter, but for a more in-depth discussion on using YAML, feel free
to look through the following Wikipedia documentation:

```
https://en.wikipedia.org/wiki/YAML
```

Command-Line Modules to Ansible Playbooks

The goal of this book is to get you working as quickly as possible, so we'll
stop the talk about syntax for the time being and get you started with a
playbook which we can easily relate back to the work we did in the first
chapter. You'll remember we installed Apache2, and then we checked if
the application was running.

We used the following commands to install Apache using the
apt module:

```
ansible mylaptop -i hosts mylaptop -m apt -a "name=apache2
state=present"
```

Even though we did not make any changes to the configuration for Apache, if we needed to configure the application, we could use the **file** module:

```
ansible mylaptop -i hosts mylaptop -m file -a "path=/tmp/
another_test owner=root group=root state=directory"
```

We were then able to ensure the Apache2 service was running using the **service** module:

```
ansible mylaptop -i hosts mylaptop -m service -a "name=apache2
state=started"
```

By using the preceding modules, we can now construct a playbook which will run through these tasks. This is a great example to start with because it will take us from the **modules** we were running on the command line to a running **playbook**.

Start by logging back into your development system, and we will get started with creating the playbook for our Apache service:

1. Start by creating a new directory where we can create our playbook. Run the following command to create the directory **test_playbooks** and will also move into the directory:

   ```
   mkdir test_playbooks; cd test_playbooks
   ```

2. Create a new hosts file in the directory we are now working in. Open the hosts file with your text editor, and make sure there is an entry for a group [webserver] as we have in the following, and feel free to add an IP address for a remote server if you are comfortable performing this installation on a remote server:

```
1 [mylaptop]
2 localhost
3
4 [webserver]
5 127.0.0.1
```

3. We can now start creating our playbook. Run the following command to create a new file called **webserver-playbook.yml** in the current directory you are working in:

touch webserver-playbook.yml

4. As we discussed earlier, we need to start our file with three dashes (---) to make sure our file is recognized as YAML file format. We will also set up the host it will deploy to; in this exercise, it will be the **webserver**:

```
1 ---
2 - hosts: webserver
```

Note   In our example, Ansible is configured to run as the **root** user and does not need to run the sudo command before it installs and makes changes to our system. If you are deploying your playbook to a host where you need to become the root user to deploy to, you will also need to use the "**become: sudo**" command after the hosts entry in our playbook. We will use the become option later on to demonstrate how this works.

---

5. Our playbook will next set up our first task to install
    Apache2 onto our system. As you can see in the
    following text, we define our plays using the word
    tasks, with all the modules we then need as part of
    our playbook listed below tasks. Enter the following
    lines into your playbook where we use the **name**
    entry in line 4 to provide a clear description of the
    task we are performing. The -name entry is not
    mandatory, and if you don't use this as part of your
    task, the module name will be output instead. Line 5
    is the same as our **apt** command-line module where
    we specify the name of the package and the state
    which defines the application version; in this case,
    we want to install **apache2** and the **version** as latest:

```
3   tasks:
4   - name: ensure apache is installed and up to date
5       apt: name=apache2 state=latest
```

6. In a real-world example, we would want to have a
    preconfigured Apache2 configuration file available
    to install onto our new system. In this exercise, we
    are simply going to use the default configuration
    file Apache2 uses as an example. Run the following
    command to obtain a copy of a default Apache2
    configuration file and place it in our current working
    directory:

```
wget https://raw.githubusercontent.com/vincesesto/
practical_ansible_ed2/main/chapter_2/test_
playbooks/000-default.conf
```

7. We can now use the **copy** module to add the
    configuration file to our webserver-playbook.yml file. You
    will also notice we have set up a **notify** action. This will
    ensure if the configuration file ever changes, Apache2 will
    be **restarted.** The value listed in line 9 specifies the name
    entry of the handler we will set up shortly:

```
6    - name: write the apache config file
7      copy: src=000-default.conf dest=/etc/apache2/
       sites-available/000-default.conf
8      notify:
9      - restart apache2
```

8. Our next task in our playbook will be to make sure
    the Apache2 service is running. Add the following
    two lines to your playbook which will use the service
    module to make sure Apache2 is running and
    enable it to start up when the system is booted:

```
10   - name: apache is running (and enable it at boot)
11     service: name=apache2 state=started enabled=yes
```

9. In lines 8 and 9 of our playbook, we specified a
    notify action to make sure Apache2 is restarted if
    there are any changes to the configuration. For this
    to work correctly, we need to set up the **handlers**
    that will respond to the "**restart apache**" action.
    Enter the following final three lines that will set up a
    new section outside our tasks, called handlers. Here,
    we specify the name and the modules to be run,
    when "**restart apache2**" is called on our playbook:

```
12   handlers:
13   - name: restart apache2
14     service: name=apache2 state=restarted
```

10. Save the playbook, and it's time to now run the playbook on our system. From the command line, in the directory where you created the **webserver-playbook.yml** file, run the following ansible-playbook command:

ansible-playbook -i hosts webserver-playbook.yml

```
PLAY [webserver] ************************************

TASK [Gathering Facts] ******************************
ok: [localhost]

TASK [ensure apache is installed and up to date]
*************
changed: [localhost]

TASK [write the apache config file] *****************
changed: [localhost]

TASK [apache is running and enable it at boot] ******
ok: [localhost]

PLAY RECAP ******************************************
localhost:
ok=5    changed=4    unreachable=0    failed=0
skipped=0    rescued=0    ignored=0
```

If it all went to plan, you should see a similar output to the preceding one where we can see the steps of each task being performed by Ansible. We can also verify we have a valid web page by going into our web browser and connecting to the IP address for our web page. If you are able to load a browser on the web system you are deploying this on, you should be able to see it by looking at the URL **http://0.0.0.0**. We should see the Apache2 welcome page similar to Figure 2-1.

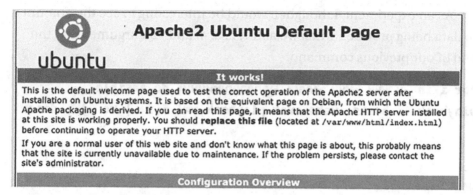

Figure 2-1. *The Apache2 Ubuntu Default Page Should Be Visible from Your Browser*

Ansible Playbook Verbose Output

The great thing about our playbook is we made sure each task had a useful and understandable description, so for each part of the output, we could see the name of each task printed to the output on the screen:

```
TASK [write the apache config file] **********************
```

When running a playbook, you will start to use the **verbose output** options available in Ansible. This involves adding a **-v** option as an argument to your command line. For example, in the previous section of this chapter, we would simply add the argument to our command like this:

```
ansible-playbook -i hosts webserver-playbook.yml -v
```

One -v argument adds the default debug output, while adding more values like **-vv** or **-vvv** or **-vvvv** will increase the amount of data being output and the detail of what is being run by Ansible. By expanding the output, we get to see the specific commands being run by the modules, and as you'll see later on, it will provide you with a good basis to troubleshoot problems with your playbooks.

As an experiment, I thought it would be interesting to see the amount of data being provided when we add 1, 2, 3, 4, and 12 v arguments to the end of our previous command:

```
for i in -v -vv -vvv -vvvv -vvvvvvvvvvvv; do ansible-
playbook -i hosts  webserver-playbook.yml ${i} | wc -l ; done
```

```
14
25
94
97
359
```

As you can see, the more v arguments we add to our command, the more data we get. When **debugging** a playbook, Ansible users will limit their output to three values (-vvv) as this generally gives enough information while not overwhelming the user with too much data.

Ansible Syntax in Finer Detail

Before we move on to our next exercise, we should go over some of the finer points in using and creating Ansible playbooks and recap what we have done in the previous section of this chapter.

Hosts and Remote Users

The **hosts** entry we made in our playbook needs to align with the inventory file we created as part of our environment. In our earlier exercise, we used the new **webserver** host we created. If we had a larger number of hosts, we could also specify the order in which we deploy to. In the following example, we are using **all** to include all of the hosts in the inventory file and the **order** of sorted, which deploys to the hosts in our inventory file in alphabetical order:

```
1 ---
2 - hosts: all
3   order: sorted
```

All is not the only value we can list for -hosts. We can also list the asterisk (*) for all; we can also specify the hostname as the host. We can list multiple hosts, separated with a colon, like localhost:127.0.0.1, or multiple groups in the same manner, such as webserver:dbserver. We can also exclude a group of hosts with an exclamation mark, such as webserver:!dbserver.

We could also set the order as **inventory**, which is the default order in our inventory file, and **reverse_inventory**, which is the reverse of the inventory order. **Sorted** will deploy to our hosts in alphabetical order and **reverse_sorted** in reverse alphabetical order, and **shuffle** will deploy in a random order to our hosts.

Our **remote user** is the user which performs the tasks; for example, we could use sudo in our project. The remote user can be defined in each of our tasks as well as at the start of the playbook. You may need to use a different user to access the system you are deploying to while needing to change to a different user to run a specific task. In the following example, we are accessing the web server as user tom, but we then need to change to the Postgres user, presumably to run database server tasks:

```
1 ---
2 - hosts: database
3   remote_user: tom
4   become: yes
5   become_user: postgres
```

In the preceding example, tom would need to have **ssh** access to the database server and be able to become the Postgres user. We are stating the method being used to perform a privileged task as follows; in this case, it is using **su**. For each of these options, such as remote_user and become, they do not need to be specified at the start of the playbook; they can also be added to each individual task if needed:

```
1 ---
2 - hosts: database
3   remote_user: tom
4   become: yes
5   become_method: su
```

We set up our servers in Chapter 1 to make sure we can both ssh and run commands as root. If you are wanting to run the playbook and have the playbook ask for a password, you can also run it with the **--ask-become-pass (or) -k** command-line argument. We will demonstrate how to use this option later in this book.

Tasks

Our Ansible playbook then took us through a list of tasks which were completed in the order they were written, one task at a time, on the host it is listed to be deployed to. Every task should include a descriptive name using the **-name** option; as we saw, this will be included as part of the ansible-playbook output:

```
3   tasks:
4   - name: ensure apache is installed and up to date
5     apt: name=apache2 state=latest
```

This was the first task we used earlier in our playbook. All our tasks are listed under the tasks statement, with a descriptive name, and the module is used to perform the task. For clarity, you may want to list all of the arguments under the module as a list. Here is an example, and it will make it easier to view multiple arguments:

```
3    tasks:
4    - name: ensure apache is installed and up to date
5      apt:
6        name=apache2
7        state=latest
```

Always make sure your whitespace is consistent as this may cause problems when your playbook is run.

Notify

We used notify in our playbook earlier in this chapter to allow our playbook to respond to changes that may be occurring in our environment. Specifically, we wanted to tell Apache2 to restart if the configuration file changes. We can set up a **notify** action at the end of a block of tasks that will only be triggered once. We could have numerous changes or tasks that could trigger a change, but Ansible will make sure to only perform this once.

The following code has been taken from our earlier playbook, where we have set up the notify in line 8 after we have performed the change to the configuration file in Apache2. We then need to set up a handler section after all the tasks for our playbook have been listed. Within the handler section, we then specify what is needed to be performed; in the following example, it is simply using the **service** module to then restart Apache2:

```
6    - name: write the apache config file
7      copy: src=000-default.conf dest=/etc/apache2/sites-
        available/000-default.conf
8      notify:
9      - restart apache
...
12   handlers:
13   - name: restart apache
14     service: name=apache2 state=restarted
```

Now that we have clarified some of the finer points of our playbook, we can move on further with our project and create a new playbook that creates a database for our LAMP stack.

Adding More Playbook Functionality with Variables and Loops

We have a nice web server up and running, but in the following exercise, we are going to add some more functionality into our playbook. As we discussed in the first chapter, the project we are currently setting up is a web server environment. We have gone about halfway so far by setting up our Apache2 server, so we can now continue to add further functionality by adding a database.

It's time for us to add this into our playbook, and we will cover off some more functionality of Ansible playbooks as we go. In the following exercise as part of creating the database server, we will define variables to be used within the playbook, and we will create loops using the with_items function to iterate over multiple values. We will introduce some new modules specific to MySQL, specifically **mysql_user** to create our root user and **mysql_db** to create databases on our server.

So, log back into your development environment, and we will get started with these changes:

1. Make sure you are in the test_playbook directory we created earlier and the web server we implemented earlier in this chapter is also running.

2. We need to make a decision first on where the database will live. Will it be on the same server as the web server or on a different host? In a production server environment, they should be separated, but for ease, we will install it on the same host our web server resides on. To do this, we will make another entry in

our hosts file, so open the file with your text editor and add in an entry for our database server. The hosts file should now look similar to the following one, but if you are wanting to add the database to the same server, feel free to add another entry with the localhost IP address:

```
1 [mylaptop]
2 localhost
3
4 [webserver]
5 127.0.0.1
6
7 [mysql]
8 <database_server_ip_address>
```

3. Create a new playbook file called **dbserver-playbook.yml** in your working directory. Use the following command to create the file from the command line:

    touch dbserver-playbook.yml

4. Open the new playbook with your text editor, and we can start to fill in the details for our new playbook. We can start with the first two lines of the playbook, adding the name of the host we are wanting to deploy our configuration management to; in this instance, it will be the mysql entry of our hosts file:

```
1 ---
2 - hosts: mysql
```

5.   We will now do something new. We are going to
     add in a **variable** into our playbook. Just as we
     created a section called tasks to list all our tasks,
     we do the same thing but call this section **vars**.
     Add the following code to create a variable named
     mysql_root_password and assign the value of
     password to it:

```
3
4   vars:
5       mysql_root_password: password
```

Note   In our playbook code, we are creating a password for our
database. This is not the best way to store passwords as it stores
them in plain text. Ansible provides a way for us to store our
passwords in a safe manner, and we will devote a large section in a
following chapter to storing passwords in a more safe manner.

---

6.   We can now start listing the tasks to create our
     database server. Our first task installs our database
     and supporting applications. To do this, we create
     our first **loop** in our playbook:

```
6 tasks:
7   - name: install mysql and python-myslqdb
8       apt: name={{ item }} update_cache=yes cache_
        valid_time=3600 state=present
9       with_items:
10      - python3-mysqldb
11      - mysql-server
```

As usual, we start the task with a descriptive name. As you will see in line 8 though, we use the **apt** module and provide **{{ item }}** as the name argument. This then refers to line 9 that uses the **with_items**, providing a list of all the applications needed to be installed as part of this task. The apt module will loop through and install all of the applications in the with_items list.

7. Next, add the following code to make sure MySQL is running. We use the shell module to run the "service mysql start" command and then ensure the service remains running on startup:

```
12    - name: start up the mysql service
13      shell: "service mysql start"
14    - name: ensure mysql is enabled to run on startup
15      service: name=mysql state=started enabled=true
```

8. Our final task will now update the mysql root passwords and grant privileges using the **mysql_user** module. For ease of reading, we have added all of the arguments for the module in a list below the **mysql_user** module from lines 16 to 22, which sets up all of the configuration items for the database user:

```
16    - name: update mysql root password for all root
        accounts
17      mysql_user:
18        name: root
19        host: "{{ item }}"
20        password: "{{ mysql_root_password }}"
21        login_user: root
```

```
22          login_password: "{{ mysql_root_password }}"
23          check_implicit_admin: yes
24          priv: "*.*:ALL,GRANT"
25            with_items:
26              - "{{ ansible_hostname }}"
27              - 127.0.0.1
28              - ::1
29              - localhost
```

We have set up a large task here which is creating the **root mysql user** on our database host using our **password** specified earlier in the playbook as a variable. It loops through the possible hostnames for our local environment to perform this change on.

9. We can now use the **mysql_db** Ansible module to create a new test database in our new database server installation. Add the following code to create the database named **testdb**, and assign it as the root user to this database:

```
30    - name: create a new database
31      mysql_db: name=testdb state=present login_
              user=root login_password="{{ mysql_root_
              password }}"
```

10. If you've worked with databases before, you might know you can create an **SQL** script that will allow you to provision the tables needed and import specific data, instead of having to perform the changes manually. Our playbook can do this by first using the **copy** module to copy the sql file into a directory on the host in line 31 and then using the **mysql_db** module again to import the sql file:

```
32   - name: add sample data to database
33     copy: src=dump.sql dest=/tmp/dump.sql
34   - name: insert sample data into database
35     mysql_db: name=testdb state=import target=/tmp/
       dump.sql login_user=root login_password="{{
       mysql_root_password }}"
```

11. Save the playbook, but before we run the playbook to deploy the new database server, we need to create the sql script that is run by the preceding code. Create the file named dump.sql in your current working directory:

    touch dump.sql

12. Open the **dump.sql** file with your text editor and add the following lines of code into the file. The following code will create a table named test and then add in some default data to the table we created:

```
1 CREATE TABLE IF NOT EXISTS test (
2   message varchar(255) NOT NULL
3 ) ENGINE=MyISAM DEFAULT CHARSET=utf8;
4 INSERT INTO test(message) VALUES('Ansible To
  Do List');
5 INSERT INTO test(message) VALUES('Get ready');
6 INSERT INTO test(message) VALUES('Ansible is fun')
```

13. If all our tasks have been set up correctly, we can now run our playbook. Run the following **ansible-playbook** command to see if your hard work has paid off:

    ansible-playbook -i hosts dbserver-playbook.yml

We have created our database and deployed it to our server and even set up our username and passwords for the default table. We can test the database to make sure our passwords are working successfully by using the **mysql** command on the command line:

```
mysql -u root -h localhost -p
Enter password:

Welcome to the MySQL monitor.  Commands end with; or \g.
...
Type 'help;' or '\h' for help. Type '\c' to clear the current
input statement.
```

If we now type "use testdb;" this should move us into the newly created database of that name:

```
mysql> use testdb;
...
Database changed
```

We can then use the "show tables;" command in mysql to see our tables:

```
mysql> show tables;
+------------------+
| Tables_in_testdb |
+------------------+
| test             |
+------------------+
1 row in set (0.00 sec)
```

Finally, we can now verify all of the data we added to our database is thereby running "**select * from test;**" as we have here:

```
mysql> select * from test;
+--------------------+
| message            |
+--------------------+
| Ansible To Do List |
| Get ready          |
| Ansible is fun     |
+--------------------+
3 rows in set (0.00 sec)
```

In a matter of minutes, we've been able to demonstrate how you can use a playbook to install and run the appropriate applications to create a database server on our system. We then configured the application to set up users and databases and should now have a full functioning and accessible database that has data preloaded into a preconfigured table.

Plugging In Our LAMP Stack

So far, we have our Linux, Apache2, and MySQL all set up for our **LAMP** stack. The last part to set up is of course the "P" which stands for either **PHP** or **Python**. We've chosen Python in this example, and we just need to make some small changes to our Apache2 web server to ensure it'll play nicely with Python scripts.

There are one or two things we need to do to allow Python to run on our Apache2 host:

- **YAML File Names End with .yml** – All our playbooks will use the .yml file name extension, and this lets everyone know it's a YAML format file.

- We need to update the **000-default.conf** file. Using Ansible, we will be able to use the file module to install it onto our environment.

- We will need to make some further changes to the Apache2 configurations in the webservice-playbopok. yml to ensure it recognizes Python and can run Python scripts. The **apache2_module** module will allow us to do that.

- We will need to use the **pip3** Ansible module to install the **pymysql** Python module.

- Finally, we need to create and install the **index.py** file, which in this instance will connect to our database and extract some data to then display on a simple web page.

Without any further delay, we should get into our working environment and link everything together:

1. You should be back in your test_playbooks directory, and for the following changes to the web server to work, you will need to make sure the database from the previous exercises is working and accessible by the web server.

2. From our working directory, we will first need to make some minor changes to the **000-default.conf** configuration file in our Apache2 installation.

3. Open the 000-default.conf file with your text editor. After the first line that will specify the **VirtualHost** for port 80, add the following five lines of configuration into your file. In the following code, we have also included the first line specifying the VirtualHost which will be left unchanged:

```
1 <VirtualHost *:80>
2
3        <Directory /var/www/test>
4            Options +ExecCGI
5            DirectoryIndex index.py
6        </Directory>
7        AddHandler cgi-script .py
```

The configuration is setting up a new directory called **/var/www/test** which will run our Python code.

4. Move further down in the 000-default.conf file and you will see a **DocumentRoot** entry; you will need to amend it to the new directory we have specified at the start of the configuration:

```
19            DocumentRoot /var/www/test
```

With the current version of Apache2, this should be around line 19 but may differ for your configuration file.

Our web server playbook already uses the 000-default.conf file as part of the installation, so we won't need to add it to the playbook.

Save this file, and if you need to get the updated version of this file from the repository, we will name it as 000-default.conf_v2, so you will know the difference.

5. We now need to make some further changes to Apache2 to get it to work nicely with Python, so open the **webservice-playbook.yml** file with your text editor to add some more functionality to it.

6. The following addition we will make will turn off multiprocessor mode and activate cgi. Make some space for the extra configuration after the last set of tasks at around line 12 and before the handler section of the playbook and add the following output:

```
12    - name: disable pmp_event on apache
13      shell: "a2dismod mpm_event"
14      notify:
15      - restart apache2
16    - name: enable cgi on apache
17      shell: "a2enmod mpm_prefork cgi"
18      notify:
19      - restart apache2
```

Notice both tasks also use the **notify** handler to let Apache2 know it requires a restart after making these changes.

Note   At the time of writing this book, there were some issues with the **apache2_module**. This module would usually give you enough functionality to make the preceding changes, but due to issues with the module not working correctly, we decided to use the **shell** commands instead.

---

7. We will add in three more tasks into our playbook before we have our handler section. Add in the following code which will install the **pymysql** Python module using the **pip3** Ansible module at line 20. We will then create the **DocumentRoot**

directory of **/var/www/test** in line 22, and the last
task will add the new index script into this directory
in line 24. Make note of the mode we need to set for
the index.py file as it needs to be executable:

```
20    - name: install pymysql module for index to use
21      pip: name=pymysql executable=pip3
22    - name: add in a test directory
23      file: path=/var/www/test/ state=directory
24    - name: add in your index file
25      copy: src=index.py dest=/var/www/test/index.py
        mode=755
26      notify:
27      - restart apache2
```

8. Your handler section should still be in place after the
    tasks you have included as part of this exercise. Your
    webserver-playbook.yml file should look like the
    following code, with all tasks running from lines 4 to
    27, with the handler section finishing up the playbook:

```
1  ---
2  - hosts: webserver
3    tasks:
4    - name: ensure apache is installed and up to date
5      apt: name=apache2 state=latest
6    - name: write the apache config file
7      copy: src=000-default.conf dest=/etc/apache2/
        sites-available/000-default.conf
8      notify:
9      - restart apache2
10   - name: apache is running and enable it at boot
11     service: name=apache2 state=started enabled=yes
```

```
12    - name: disable pmp_event on apache
13      shell: "a2dismod mpm_event"
14      notify:
15      - restart apache2
16    - name: enable cgi on apache
17      shell: "a2enmod mpm_prefork cgi"
18      notify:
19      - restart apache2
20    - name: install pymysql module for index to use
21      pip: name=pymysql executable=pip3
22    - name: add in a test directory
23      file: path=/var/www/test/ state=directory
24    - name: add in your index file
25      copy: src=index.py dest=/var/www/test/index.py
        mode=755
26      notify:
27      - restart apache2
28    handlers:
29    - name: restart apache2
30      service: name=apache2 state=restarted
31
```

If you need to refer to this code in the GitHub repository, this code will be in the file called **webserver-playbook-v2.yml**.

9. We now need to create the **index.py** file that we are now referring to in our playbook, so create a file called index.py in your current working directory where your playbooks are located:

touch index.py

10. Open the new index.py file with your text editor and add the following code. We are not going to go too much in depth as to what this script does, but to quickly explain, we import our Python modules, connect to the database, and then print out all of the data in the new tables we created:

```
1 #!/usr/bin/python3
2
3 import pymysql
4
5 # Print necessary headers.
6 print("Content-Type: text/html")
7 print()
8
9 # Connect to the database.
10 conn = pymysql.connect(
11                 db='testdb',
12                 user='root',
13                 passwd='password',
14                 host='localhost')
15 c = conn.cursor()
16
17 # Print the contents of the table.
18 c.execute("SELECT * FROM test;")
19 for i in c:
20     print(i)
```

11. Save the changes you have made to the index.py file, and just before we run out of playbook again, let's make sure we have all our files. In our current working directory, we should have the following list of files:

   a. **001-default.conf** – The new Apache2 configuration file to be deployed and now allowing the ability for the application to interact with Python and the database we have created

   b. **dbserver-playbook.yml** – The playbook that manages configurations of our database server

   c. **dump.sql** – The SQL file that creates our default database and table and adds in additional data

   d. **hosts** – The lists hosts Ansible is using to deploy to

   e. **index.py** – Our web server index file to display content from the database

   f. **webserver-playbook.yml** – The Ansible playbook that manages the configuration of our web server

12. Our webserver-playbook.yml is ready to be deployed. We have set this up to run and install our web server from a new installation, or it will update an established installation. Run the following ansible-playbook command to hopefully have all our configuration complete:

```
ansible-playbook -i hosts webserver-playbook.yml
```

Once the playbook runs, you will now be able to log into your web page with the IP address of the webserver. As the **DocumentRoot** has been set up, you will not need to specify the path; simply place your IP address into your web browser, and you should see the image shown in Figure 2-2.

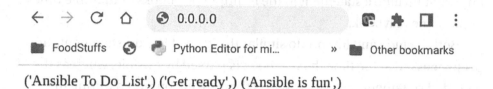

('Ansible To Do List',) ('Get ready',) ('Ansible is fun',)

Figure 2-2. *The New Web Page Visible from Your Browser*

It is really not very interesting, but you need to remember, in a short amount of time, you have been able to set up code to create and provision your database server, create the database and user, and add default data and tables to the database. We then set up a web server with Python3 support that can interact with our database and connect and extract data and serve to a web page. Although we have finished working on our LAMP stack for this part of the chapter, continue on as the following section will discuss how you can start to reuse your code and playbooks.

Organizing Larger Playbooks with Include and Import

At this time, you're probably seeing the benefit of using a playbook but wondering how they work when the deployments and environments you're creating and supporting become more complex. The way our current playbooks stand, as our environment continues to grow, our playbooks would also continue to grow. But there are a few things we can do to organize things better and ensure our playbooks remain readable and don't get overly complex. In the next few pages, we will introduce you to **include** and **import**.

Both include and import would be familiar to you if you have some background in programming. In Ansible, they work in a similar way and allow us to start to make our playbooks more reusable and modular. Tasks are separated out from the main playbook and are then referred to with an import or include a statement in the multiple playbooks or multiple times in the same playbook.

Both include and import do similar things, but import statements are **preprocessed** at the time the playbook is parsed by Ansible, whereas the included statements are processed as they are encountered during the **execution** of the playbook.

Note   Please make note if you are using or working with an older version of Ansible. Prior to version 2.4, only include statements were available. If you use an import in these earlier versions, you will be met with an error when running your Ansible playbook.

To clarify how import and include work is, we are going to make a small change to the work we were looking at earlier in the chapter. We will create a new playbook that uses import to use both the webserver-playbook.yml and dbserver-playbook.yml as part of its own playbook to deploy our configurations:

1. Log back into your work environment and move into the directory you've been working in to create the database and web server.

2. Use the following touch command to create the playbook called new-playbook.yml:

   ```
   touch new-playbook.yml
   ```

3. Open the new playbook with your text editor and add in the following code. As you can see, there is not too much involved, but by using the **import_ playbook** commands, we can import both of our previous playbooks into this one:

```
1 ---
2 - import_playbook: webserver-playbook.yml
3 - import_playbook: dbserver-playbook.yml
```

4. That's all there is to it. We've created a new playbook and reused the playbooks we created earlier in the chapter. Save the file and you can now run it with the following command:

```
ansible-playbook -i hosts new-playbook.yml
```

If all goes well, you should see a very similar output to what you saw when you ran each of your playbooks separately with the imported playbooks being deployed in the order they were specified in the new-playbook.yml file.

Instead of importing a playbook, you could create a list of common tasks which are used as part of your deployment. Your playbook running the common tasks would then use include or import tasks to use them.

As an example, we are using handlers to signal a restart of Apache2 if the configurations have changed. We could create a file called **apache_ handlers.yml** and add in the following tasks to simply do this one task:

```
---
- name: restart apache2
  service: name=apache2 state=restarted
```

In our webserver playbook file, we would then use import or include to refer to the tasks we have created earlier:

```
handlers:
- include_tasks: apache_handlers.yml
# or
- import_tasks: apache_handlers.yml
```

As long as our notify statement is using the correct task name of "restart apache2," the handler will work correctly.

Note   Although import and include statements are important parts of using Ansible within playbooks, the use of these statements is limited with more users opting to use **roles** to organize their playbook structure. Our focus will now move to roles in the next chapter, and we will not have much more exposure to import and include statements.

Summary

I hope you are finding this book interesting and challenging. We've done a lot of work in this chapter and covered a lot of ground. We started by taking a look at YAML and how we can set up our Ansible playbooks and then moved on to taking our command-line modules into our first real playbook. We then developed our skills and our LAMP stack further with a MySQL database and then Python support, all the while discussing what the different syntax of the playbooks mean.

Finally, we take a look at how we organize our playbooks and think about how we can make them more manageable and reusable. This is the theme we take forward into our next chapter as we introduce roles to organize our playbooks into a universal structure. At the same time, we will take this further by putting more features into our LAMP stack.

## CHAPTER 3

Extending Playbooks with Roles and Templates

At the end of the last chapter, we had a quick look at how we can start to organize our playbooks to allow them to grow while still being able to keep some control over how they're organized. We discussed how you can use import and include as part of our playbooks to use and reuse other playbooks we have created previously within new playbooks.

This may not seem too important now, but our environment only consists of two servers currently. What we need is a standard way to organize each piece of our environment so we're able to make smaller and simpler pieces of configuration syntax and items. What if we took this further and wanted to not only reuse our code and configurations but wanted to share our configurations with other people and, in return, use configurations other people have written? Well, you've come to the right place. Ansible provides you with an easy way to do this with the use of **roles**.

We felt roles were so useful that we needed to dedicate an entire chapter to them and how we can incorporate them into our project. In this chapter

© Vincent Sesto 2022

V. Sesto, *Practical Ansible*, https://doi.org/10.1007/978-1-4842-8643-2_3

- We will introduce roles and start by incorporating them into our LAMP stack project to show you how they are organized and used.

- We will give you a breakdown of the directory structure and how to make best use of setting up your playbooks with them.

- We will extend our project further and introduce **Django** into our LAMP stack.

- We will start to use **command-line arguments** and variables to allow more flexibility when we are deploying our code.

- We will introduce **conditionals** and **tags** into our playbooks to allow us to increase the functionality and allow only specific parts of our playbook to run.

We previously saw how we can start to reuse our code, but the following chapter will show you how we can take this further to organize our playbooks and configuration management even further.

Ansible Roles

Out of the two ways that Ansible is able to reuse our configuration management tasks within playbooks, we have already discussed the first way by using import and include. The second way of reusing our tasks is through roles. Both work in a similar way, but roles allow you a lot more flexibility. Instead of simply packaging tasks together, roles allow you to set up a specific structure to include **variables**, **handlers**, **modules**, and other plugins, all of which can be uploaded to **Ansible Galaxy** which is a central repository or hub for sharing, finding, and reusing your Ansible code (but more on that later in the chapter).

In the following section, you will see how we can use roles to break up our configuration into more modular steps. The directory structure we will set up will be similar across all roles, allowing us to be consistent and not need to create our own formula for organizing the configuration.

Creating the Web Server Role

We are going to start working with the web server playbook we have created in the previous chapter. We are going to take the existing playbook and break it up and turn it into an Ansible role for us to then deploy and redeploy when you need to.

Log into your working environment and access the test_playbook directory where we have all of our previous work located:

1. From within the directory we have been working on, you should be able to perform a listing of the files in the directory, and you should have the following files in there:

    a. **000-default.conf** – The Apache2 configuration file

    b. **dbserver-playbook.yml** – The playbook that manages configurations of our database server

    c. **dump.sql** – The SQL file that creates our default database and table and adds in additional data

    d. **hosts** – The lists hosts Ansible is using to deploy to

    e. **index.py** – Our web server index file to display content from the database

    f. **webserver-playbook.yml** – The Ansible playbook that manages the configuration of our web server

2. To start the process of creating our web server, we need a directory to store our roles, so create the new directory with the following command:

    mkdir roles

3. Within our roles directory, we are going to create our first role; in this instance, we are going to call it **web_server**. To create this new role, we simply create a new directory for the role to live in:

    mkdir roles/web_server

4. For each role we create, there are a standard set of directories we need to include to house our data; these are

    a. **Files** – This includes all our supporting files. In our example, this might include configuration files.

    b. **Handlers** – As we saw in our playbooks, we can set up handlers to perform specific tasks upon completion of our playbook. This is the separate directory for the handlers.

    c. **Meta** – This is for files to establish role dependencies or roles that need to be applied before your current role can work correctly.

    d. **Templates** – Instead of needing a separate file for all different web servers, you may be able to set up a template to cover them all. We will be discussing templates later in the book.

    e. **Tasks** – These are simply the tasks in our playbook to get our role to a specific state. Just as we created the tasks in our playbooks earlier, we will separate our tasks and place them in their own directory.

f. **Vars** – These are variables that can be included as part of our tasks.

g. **Defaults** – These are default variables for our roles.

To get our new role started, run the following commands to create all of the directories for our web_server role. Even if we don't use all of the directories, it is good to have them all in place as these are the standard directories used for roles:

```
mkdir -p roles/web_server/{files,handlers,meta,
templates,tasks,vars,defaults}
```

5. We can now start to convert our webserver-playbook.yml file into a role. We will start by moving all of the tasks in our playbook into the **tasks** directory. Run the following command to copy the original playbook into the tasks directory, and we are going to call the file **mail.yml**:

```
cp webserver-playbook.yml roles/web_server/tasks/
main.yml
```

6. Open the roles/web_server/tasks/main.yml file with your text editor and change the file to remove anything which is not a task. This means we need to remove the hosts details and notifiers section in the playbook, and it should now look like as follows:

```
1 ---
2 - name: ensure apache is installed and up to date
3    apt: name=apache2 state=latest
4 - name: write the apache config file
5    copy: src=000-default.conf dest=/etc/apache2/
     sites-available/000-default.conf
```

```
 6   notify:
 7    - restart apache2
 8  - name: apache is running and enable it at boot
 9    service: name=apache2 state=started enabled=yes
10  - name: disable pmp_event on apache
11    shell: "a2dismod mpm_event"
12    notify:
13    - restart apache2
14  - name: enable cgi on apache
15    shell: "a2enmod mpm_prefork cgi"
16    notify:
17    - restart apache2
18  - name: install pymysql module for index to use
19    pip: name=pymysql executable=pip3
20  - name: add in a test directory
21    file: path=/var/www/test/ state=directory
22  - name: add in your index file
23    copy: src=index.py dest=/var/www/test/index.py
      mode=755
24    notify:
25    - restart apache2
```

As you can see, we have removed the handlers and
the host details at the start of the file. Make sure you
include the three dashes at the start of the file and
all indent points are brought in closer to the left of
the file.

7.   The file we created in the previous step refers to **src**
files used as part of the web server configuration.
This includes both the **000-default.conf** and **index.
py** files used as part of our web server playbook.
Ansible will know all of these **src** files are located

in the **files** directory of our web_server role, so we can move them over to this directory now with the following command:

```
cp 000-default.conf roles/web_server/files/
cp index.py roles/web_server/files/
```

8. We can now move the handlers from our webserver_playbook.yml file. Start by creating the new handlers file named main.yml in the roles/web_server/handlers/ directory as we have here:

```
touch roles/web_server/handlers/main.yml
```

9. We only have one handler set up in our playbook, so open the new file we created with your text editor and enter in the following three lines to set it up:

```
1 ---
2 - name: restart apache2
3   service: name=apache2 state=restarted
```

10. After all the work we've done, we need some way to now run the web_server role we have created. To do this, we simply create a separate playbook to run the role we have created. We will call the new playbook to run our role site.yml:

```
touch site.yml
```

11. Open the new playbook with your text editor and add in the following text to run our new web_server role:

```
1 ---
2 - hosts: webserver
```

```
3  roles:
4      - web_server
```

Instead of having a list of tasks in our playbook, we now list in lines 3 and 4 the roles we want to run as part of our playbook.

12. We can see the directory structure clearly by running the **tree** command if you have this available on your system. We have run the given command to provide the following output with our original playbook tasks in the tasks directory, the handlers in their own directory, and supporting configuration documents like the index.py script and the Apache2 configuration in the files directory:

tree roles/web_server/

```
roles/web_server/
|-- defaults
|-- files
|   |-- 000-default.conf
|   `-- index.py
|-- handlers
|   `-- main.yml
|-- meta
|-- tasks
|   `-- main.yml
|-- templates
`-- vars
```

To run the playbook, we do the same thing we've been doing earlier, but this time, we use the **site.yml** file as our playbook:

```
ansible-playbook -i hosts site.yml
```

13. Although there are no real changes to our environment, the playbook will run happily and find all its relevant information in the roles directory structure. If you really wanted to test this, you could remove the Apache2 server first before running the playbook again:

```
sudo apt-get remove --purge $(dpkg -l apache* |
grep ii | awk '{print $2}')
```

Even though our **site.yml** file looks a lot more sparse than what our previous playbooks did, all the magic happens here through the use of the roles statement. By using our roles statement, we no longer need to refer to imported or included YAML files as our role will already know where to find everything it needs.

As in our project, all Ansible roles are implemented with the same behavior. The tasks needed to create role will work through the following directories in order:

- tasks
- handlers
- vars
- defaults
- meta

Ansible pieces our playbook together as if we had been using our original web server playbook. Now that we have the web service running as a role, let's move onto the next section where we break down our dbserver-playbook.yml into its own Ansible role.

Creating the Database Server Role

With everything we've just learned, we should be able to breeze through turning our **dbserver-playbook.yml** into an Ansible role that can be used in the **site.yml** playbook. If you are no longer in your working environment, log back in so we can get started with creating our next Ansible role:

1. We already have our roles directory set up from the previous exercise, but we will first need to create a directory for our new database server role. Perform the following command to create the directory **db_server**:

    ```
    mkdir roles/db_server
    ```

2. Now, run the following seven commands to create the files, handlers, meta, templates, tasks, and vars directories in our new db_server role:

    ```
    mkdir -p roles/db_server/{files,handlers,meta,
    templates,tasks,vars,defaults}
    ```

Note   The creation of all these directories seems a little redundant, and don't worry, in the next chapter, we will show you how to set up your roles without having to manually create all the directories. For now, we are doing this to help you get used to where everything is located in our role.

---

3. As we did with our previous section of this chapter,
    we can start by setting up the tasks for our db_server
    role. We do this by copying our original database
    playbook into the tasks directory and rename it to
    main.yml:

    cp dbserver-playbook.yml roles/db_server/tasks/main.yml

4. We can now trim down the file and remove anything
    we no longer need. This will be the first six lines at
    the top of the file including the variables, as we have
    somewhere to place them in our roles directory
    structure. Our main.yml tasks file should look
    similar to the following file:

```
1 ---
2 - name: install mysql and python-myslqdb
3   apt: name={{ item }} update_cache=yes cache_valid_
      time=3600 state=present
4   with_items:
5   - python3-mysqldb
6   - mysql-server
7 - name: start up the mysql service
8   shell: "service mysql start"
9 - name: ensure mysql is enabled to run on startup
10  service: name=mysql state=started enabled=true
11 - name: update mysql root password for all root
      accounts
12  mysql_user:
13    name: root
14    host: "{{ item }}"
15    login_unix_socket: /var/run/mysqld/mysqld.sock
16    password: "{{ mysql_root_password }}"
17    login_user: root
```

```
18      login_password: "{{ mysql_root_password }}"
19      check_implicit_admin: yes
20      priv: "*.*:ALL,GRANT"
21   with_items:
22      - "{{ ansible_hostname }}"
23      - 127.0.0.1
24      - ::1
25      - localhost
26 - name: create a new database
27   mysql_db: name=testdb state=present login_
     user=root login_password="{{ mysql_root_
     password }}"
28 - name: add sample data to database
29   copy: src=dump.sql dest=/tmp/dump.sql
30 - name: insert sample data into database
31   mysql_db: name=testdb state=import target=/tmp/
     dump.sql login_user=root login_password="{{ mysql_
     root_password }}"
```

5. We don't have any handlers in our original playbook,
    but we do have a **variable** section for the database
    password. We can add this to our **vars** directory that
    is set up as part of our roles. Create the main.yml file
    in the vars directory with the following command:

touch roles/db_server/vars/main.yml

6. Open the main.yml file we have just created in the
    vars directory with your text editor. We only have
    one variable so far, so add the following two lines
    into the file and save it:

```
1 ---
2 mysql_root_password: password
```

7. Lastly, we need to add the **dump.sql** file into the files directory of our new db_server role, which performs the job of creating our sample tables and data in our database. Run the following command to copy it into the **files** directory:

```
cp dump.sql roles/db_server/files/
```

8. With the new db_server role created, we can now add it to our **site.yml** file. We will deploy both roles to the same system, so update the site.yml file to look like the following output:

```
1 ---
2 - hosts: webserver
3   roles:
4     - web_server
5     - db_server
```

9. Once again, we can run the playbook with the command we used earlier; this time, it will deploy both the web_server and db_server roles:

```
ansible-playbook -i hosts site.yml
```

10. If the preceding ansible-playbook command runs without any errors, our deployment should have been successful. Finally, we can do some cleanup and remove all of the files in our current directory

we are no longer using as they have now been
placed into their appropriate roles directories for
either the web_server or db_server run. Run the
following command to clean up the unwanted files:

```
rm 000-default.conf dbserver-playbook.yml dump.sql
hosts index.py webserver-playbook.yml
```

The only files remaining in our working directory should be our
hosts file, the new **site.yml** playbook, and the **roles** directory, which now
includes our new database and web server roles.

You have made a lot of changes to your environment, so make sure
you continue to commit your changes to your GitHub repository before
moving on. The next section of this chapter will discuss using extra options
and variables we can use as part of the ansible-playbook command to help
with our deployments.

Ansible Command-Line Variables and Options

In our example project we have been working on, we used the vars
directory as part of our role to define a variable to be used by our playbook.
We won't dwell too long on this, but you can also provide an overriding
variable as part of your command-line arguments. In the next section of
this chapter, we will use the **--extra-vars** option or the **-e** option to provide
variables when we run our command in the console. This is a good way
to test variables before placing them in the vars directory or if you need
to override any of the variables currently in place. When you use the
environment variables option, you then need to specify the name of the
variable and then the value it is equal to, for example:

```
--extra-vars variable=test
-e variable=test
```

You need to specify the option for each extra variable you wish to define, or you can include them in inverted commas as listed like the one as follows:

```
-e "variable1=test1 variable2=test2"
```

You will need to remember there is a precedence and order from which Ansible will take its variables from. For now, all you need to know is if you place variables in the command line with the --extra-vars option, they will override any other variables you have in your Ansible role.

For now, if you are going to store them as part of your role, make sure they are either in the defaults directory or in the vars directory (vars will override defaults). If you would like a full and detailed list of variable precedence, go to the following location in the Ansible documentation:

```
http://docs.ansible.com/ansible/latest/playbooks_variables.
html#variable-precedence-where-should-i-put-a-variable
```

Expanding Our LAMP with Django

In our first chapter, we discussed this project was going to incorporate Django as part of our environment. I know we're almost through our third chapter, but we are now going to set up Django and allow it to use our MySQL database to store data, and then we can have Apache2 host the services.

As we discussed in our first chapter, we are not going to go too far in depth with Django, so we will walk through all of the concepts as we go. Of course, we are going to create a role as we set it up to make sure it is in line with the work we are currently doing.

Note   Django is a Python-based web framework that allows programmers to create fully functioning websites quickly without needing to sort out the finer details of how it will scale or worry about security. Django is open source, and there is a lot of information on the Web on how to use and create applications. One of the best places to start is from the link `www.djangoproject.com/`.

Log back into your development environment, and access the directory you have been working in previously to get started:

1.   The first thing we will need to do is create a new role for Django. Run the following command to create the new role called **django_app**:

```
mkdir roles/django_app
```

2.   Just as we have done so with the database and Apache2 roles we created, it's time to create all the supporting directories which will be part of our role. Run the following commands to create all the supporting directories:

```
mkdir -p roles/django_app/{defaults,files,handlers,
meta,tasks,templates,vars}
```

3.   We can start by setting up the tasks we need to perform to create our Django environment. We have not created a playbook for this yet, so we will be starting from scratch. Run the following command to create the **main.yml** file in our tasks directory:

```
touch roles/django_app/tasks/main.yml
```

4. Open the main.yml file with your text editor and start by creating the following two tasks, where we install the latest version of **python3-django** and create a directory where our application will be created in:

```
1 ---
2 - name: install django and make sure it is at the
     latest version
3   apt: name=python3-django state=present
4 - name: create a directory for our django app
5   file: path={{ django_app_location }}/web_app
     mode=0755 owner=root group=root state=directory
```

We are using the variable **django_app_location** which we will specify in the command line. Line 3 uses the **apt** module to install the latest version of python3-django, and line 5 uses the **file** module to create the application directory for our **web_app**.

Note   We are using the owner and group value of **user**. You need to make sure your code includes a valid user on the system you are running your playbook code on.

---

5. Stay in the same file; we now need to create a new Django application using the **django-admin** command. Add the following code to the file where line 7 uses the **shell** module to perform the

django-admin command to create our new app, and line 9 uses the **copy** module to add in our application configuration:

```
6 - name: create your new django app in the
    web_app directory
7   shell: django-admin startproject web_app
    {{ django_app_location }}/web_app
8 - name: configure your database to use work
    with django
9   copy: src=settings.py dest={{ django_app_location
    }}/web_app/web_app/settings.py
```

6. Continue to add the following tasks to our role. Line 11 uses the shell module again to run the Django **manage.py** script to set up our database:

```
10 - name: apply a migration into the mysql database
11   shell: python3 {{ django_app_location }}/web_app/
     manage.py migrate
```

7. Line 13 is pretty involved as it runs a command to create the new **superuser** administrator for our web_app as well as setting the credentials including the password for the user. The command sets the admin user password to 'changeme'. This can be changed to something you feel is more secure, or you can change the password later once Django has been installed and is available:

```
12 - name: populate admin with password
13   shell: python3 {{ django_app_location }}
     /web_app/manage.py shell -c "from django.
     contrib.auth.models import User; User.objects.
     filter(username='admin').exists() or User.objects.
     create_superuser('admin','admin@example.com',
     'changeme')"
```

8. This should be everything we currently need to include in our django_app tasks, so make sure all the changes have been saved and close the main. yml file for now.

9. In lines 8 and 9 of our django_app tasks, we are adding a preconfigured **settings.py** file to our configuration. We will need to create this and place it in the roles/django_app/files/ directory. You will be able to download a sample version from the authors GitHub repository. Use the following wget command to extract the file from GitHub, and then place it in the roles/django_app/files directory of our role:

```
wget https://raw.githubusercontent.com/vincesesto/
practical_ansible_ed2/main/chapter_3/test_playbooks/
roles/django_app/files/settings.py roles/django_app/
files/settings.py
```

10. If you haven't worked with Django before, you may not know the settings.py file will be configured to use **SQLite** database to work with upon installation. We already have a MySQL database which we set up earlier, so a configuration change is needed to ensure it can be used as part of this project.

91

The only difference to the default version we have downloaded as part of the previous is from line 76, which has our MySQL database details added instead of the SQLite details. Using your text editor, open the settings.py file in the roles/django_app/ files/ directory and make sure these lines should look similar to the following ones:

```
76 DATABASES = {
77     'default': {
78         'ENGINE': 'django.db.backends.mysql',
79         'NAME': 'web_app',
80         'USER': 'root',
81         'PASSWORD': 'password',
82         'HOST': 'localhost',
83         'PORT': '',
84     }
85 }
```

11. While you have the settings file open, if you are using a web browser on the system you are working on, you might need to add your IP address to the ALLOWED_HOSTS value. It will be set to an empty list, but move through the file, most likely around line 28, and make sure your IP address is added as we have here:

```
28 ALLOWED_HOSTS = ['0.0.0.0']
```

12. Save the settings.py file, as our django_app role should now be complete, but we need to make an additional change to our db_server role first.

13. Open the roles/db_server/tasks/main.yml file
    with your text editor and change the tasks that
    create the database for us. This should be at line 26
    where the name of the database will now reflect the
    information we have set in our Django settings.py
    file. Make the following change to set the name as
    equal to web_app:

```
25 - name: create a new database
26    mysql_db: name=web_app state=present login_
      user=root login_password="{{ mysql_root_
      password }}
```

14. Now we need to add the django_app role into our
    site.yml file to make sure it's installed as part of our
    environment. Open the site.yml file, and it should
    now have the django_app role added and look
    similar to the following output:

```
1 ---
2 - hosts: webserver
3   roles:
4       - web_server
5       - db_server
6       - django_app
```

15. You may be wondering when we are going to set up
    the **django_app_location** variable we are using in
    our django_app tasks. But with our new knowledge
    of command-line arguments, we will add it now
    when we run our Ansible playbook command.
    Run the following command using the --extra-vars
    option to specify the location where our app will be

located. In the following instance, we are using the current working directory with the `pwd` command. Make sure you are using backticks in the following command and not inverted commas:

```
ansible-playbook -i hosts site.yml --extra-vars
django_app_location=`pwd`
```

16. We can now test our server with the built-in web server Django provides. We will configure it to work with Apache2 later in this chapter, but for now, we will use this to verify all our changes have worked correctly. Run the test web server with the following command:

```
python3 web_app/manage.py runserver 0.0.0.0:8000

Performing system checks...
System check identified no issues (0 silenced).
March 23, 2018 - 03:08:45
Django version 1.11.4, using settings 'web_app.
settings'
Starting development server at http://0.0.0.0:8000/
Quit the server with CONTROL-C.
```

Note   We have used port 8000 to run the Django test server. This needs to be different from the port Apache2 is running, which would be running on port 80.

If you have a web browser running on your environment, you will now be able to test the environment by entering the following domain: **http://localhost:8000/**. You'll see something like Figure 3-1.

django
View release notes for Django 2.2

The install worked successfully! Congratulations!

You are seeing this page because DEBUG=True is in your
settings file and you have not configured any URLs.

Figure 3-1. *The Django Welcome Page from Your Web Browser*

Or we can test our administration page with **http://localhost:8000/
admin** (Figure 3-2).

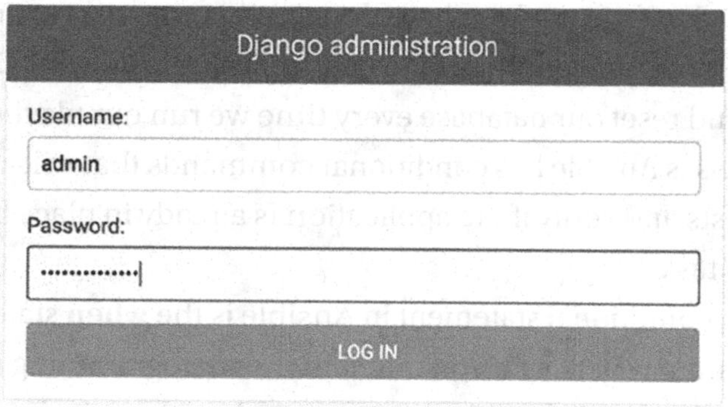

Django administration
Username:
admin
Password:
•••••••••••••|
LOG IN

Figure 3-2. *The Django Admin Login Page*

If everything has worked correctly, the admin domain should look
similar to the preceding image, and we should be able to log in with the
admin username and the password we created as part of our django_app
playbook.

The playbook we set up does the job of implementing the admin superuser upon installation. If you need to change the password for this user, you can run the following command from your working directory to perform the changepassword command:

```
python3 web_app/manage.py changepassword admin
```

```
Changing password for user 'admin'
Password:
Password (again):
Password changed successfully for user 'admin'
```

For now, our roles are coming along well, but the following section will look at adding extra functionality to our roles through the use of conditional statements.

Conditional Tasks in Ansible

Before we finish off the work we have done in this chapter, we need to highlight one point. We don't want to continually reinstall our Django application and reset our database every time we run our playbook. The good news is Ansible has conditional commands that will allow us to perform tests and verify if the application is already in place before performing a task.

The main conditional statement in Ansible is the **when** statement and works in a similar way to an **if** statement in most programming languages. For our example, we will be able to create a task to check if our application directory exists; we can then make sure our Django commands and database migrations are only performed when the Django application has not been previously created.

Let's get back into our working environment, and we can implement this with only a few minor changes to our django_app role:

1. We will need to make changes to the tasks we have previously created, so use your text editor to open the tasks file for the django_app role under **roles/ django_app/tasks/main.yml**.

2. The first two tasks we perform are to install Django and then create the application directory. We can place our installation test just after this at line 6, so add the following four lines to our list of tasks:

```
4 - name: check if django app already exists
5   shell: ls -l {{ django_app_location }} |
      grep -c web_app
6   register: djangostatus
7   failed_when: djangostatus.rc == 2
```

The preceding code performs a simple shell command to test if the application directory called **web_app** has been created or not. It then creates the **djangostatus** value using the **register** statement and will fail if the returned value is equal to 2. If the application is present, it will be assigned as 1, and if not, it will have the value of 0.

Note   Ansible allows you to define what a failure is for each task. In the preceding example, we are using the **failed_when** statement to set our failure to be when the dbstatus value is equal to 2. This should only happen if the task performing the directory listing actually fails.

---

3. The remaining tasks can then be amended to have
    the when statement for each of them as we have
    listed them as follows. Add in the following code; we
    have highlighted the additional statements in bold
    and will only run these specific tasks if the result of
    our django directory test or djangostatus is "0" or
    not present:

Note   We have included a second file in our repository called
main-v2.yml that includes all of the following changes, as well as the
tags we will also introduce shortly.

```
08 - name: create a directory for our django app
09   file: path={{ django_app_location }}/web_app
        mode=0755 owner=user group=user state=directory
10   when: djangostatus.stdout == "0"
11 - name: create your new django app in the web_app
        directory
12   shell: django-admin startproject web_app {{
        django_app_location }}web_app
13   when: djangostatus.stdout == "0"
14 - name: configure your database to use work
        with django
15   copy: src=settings.py dest={{ django_app_location
        }}/web_app/web_app/settings.py
16   when: djangostatus.stdout == "0"
17 - name: apply a migration into the mysql database
18   shell: python3 {{ django_app_location }}/web_app/
        manage.py migrate
19   when: djangostatus.stdout == "0"
```

```
20 - name: create the admin superuser
21   shell: python3 {{ django_app_location }}/web_app/
     manage.py createsuperuser --noinput --username=
     admin --email=admin@example.com
22   when: djangostatus.stdout == "0"
```

4. We can now run our playbook the same way we did
   earlier:

**ansible-playbook -i hosts site.yml -e django_app_
location=`pwd`**

If you have previously installed Django and have the application
directory already created, we should see our output skipping the tasks
we put in place in the django_app role. The recap displayed when the
playbook has completed should also show the number of skipped tasks, in
our case 5:

```
TASK [django_app : create your new django app in the web_app
directory] ********************************
skipping: [localhost]
TASK [django_app : configure your database to use work with
django] ************************************
skipping: [localhost]
TASK [django_app : apply a migration into the mysql database]
******************************************
skipping: [localhost]
TASK [django_app : populate admin with password] *************
**********************************
skipping: [localhost]
RUNNING HANDLER [web_server : restart apache2] ***************
********************************
changed: [localhost]
```

```
PLAY RECAP  ************************************************
*****************************
127.0.0.1                      : ok=19    changed=7    unreachable=0
failed=0    skipped=5    rescued=0    ignored=0
```

Using conditional tasks in your playbooks and roles is an easy way to control the flow of what needs to be run and what doesn't. In the next section, we will demonstrate how you can implement tags as part of your playbooks to achieve a similar way to control the flow of your work.

Using Tags to Run Specific Tasks

We have just used conditionals to run specific parts of our playbook when needed, but we can also use **tags** within our playbook to limit what is run and what isn't run when we perform a deployment. All we need to do in our code is to mark it with the tags attribute, and this will allow us to then call these specific tags when we run the playbook.

In the previous section, we have used the when statement to make sure only certain tasks in a playbook are run if Django has been previously installed. In the following section, we will make a minor amendment to our role to allow us to call one specific task if we need it.

You can add tags to any part of your deployment, but they will only affect tasks, and it can help you by adding the tag to the role; the tag will then be applied to all the tasks in the role.

As we've seen, the best way to explain how features work is by adding it into the code, so log back into your working environment and we will do some minor work to the **django_app** role to demonstrate how we can start to work with tags:

1. We will need to make a new change to the **roles/ django_app/tasks/main.yml** file, so open this file with your text editor ready to make changes.

2. We are going to make a minor change to the first
    task in our playbook, so add an extra line to the first
    task as we have here, adding in the **tags: django_
    alive** entry in line 4:

```
1 ---
2 - name: install django and make sure it is at the
    latest version
3   apt: name=python3-django state=present
4   tags: django_alive
```

3. We can now verify we have set up the tags correctly
    by running the playbook, but adding the **--list-tags**
    option at the end of the command. This will only
    list all the tags we have added to our roles without
    running the playbooks and should look similar to
    the following output:

ansible-playbook -i hosts site.yml -e django_app_
location=`pwd` --list-tags
```
playbook: site.yml

  play #1 (webserver): webserver          TAGS: []
      TASK TAGS: [django_present]
```

As you can see, in all of our roles the site.yml file
runs, there is only one tag set up in play #1.

4. We will now amend tags to our site.yml file to
    demonstrate how these will affect all the tasks in the
    role. Open the **site.yml** file with your text editor to
    get this started.

5. We will set up a tag in the site.yml file to only deploy the database if needed. Amend the file to now look like the following. As you can see, we have needed to make a slight change to the structure of the file to make sure the tag of deploy_database_only can be applied:

```
1 ---
2 - hosts: webserver
3   roles:
4   - web_server
5   - role: db_server
6     tags: ['deploy_database_only']
7   - django_app
```

6. To now run our playbook and only deploy the database, we simply use the **--tags** option and the tag we created earlier. Run the following command to perform this exact change:

**ansible-playbook -i hosts site.yml -e django_app_
location=`pwd` --tags deploy_database_only**

Ansible comes with a tag you can add to make sure a specific task is always run, and of course, it is called **always.** Tasks with this tag will be run every time you run your playbook unless you use the **--skip-tags** option in your ansible command.

7. Open the site.yml file once again, and we will demonstrate how to use the always tag with our current project.

8. Change lines 7 and 8 of the site.yml file to look the
    same as the following code. We might determine the
    Django app is of high priority and needs to always
    be deployed whenever we run the site.yml playbook.
    The following changes amend the django_app role
    being called to have the tag set to always. Save the
    file ready to test:

```
1 ---
2 - hosts: webserver
3   roles:
4     - web_server
5     - role: db_server
6       tags: ['deploy_database_only']
7     - role: django_app
8       tags: ['always']
```

Note   The preceding code is also listed in our repository as site-v2.
yml, which includes the latest update that includes tags.

---

9. Before we run our playbook, use the **--list-tags**
    option again to view the tags we have across all
    our roles that are being used. As you can see from
    the following output, we now have three tags listed
    across the roles being used:

```
ansible-playbook -i hosts site.yml -e django_app_
location=`pwd` --list-tags
playbook: site.yml
  play #1 (webserver): webserver TAGS: []
      TASK TAGS: [always, deploy_database_only,
      django_alive]
```

10. Run the playbook again as we did earlier, only using the **deploy_database_only** tag. Although the **db_server** role is run, the **django_app** role is also run because it is tagged with the always tag:

```
ansible-playbook -i hosts site.yml -e django_app_
location=`pwd` --tags deploy_database_only
```

This brings us to the end of the exercises for this chapter. Hopefully, you can see the benefits of using roles in your configuration management process and can see how tags can also simplify and change the way our playbooks run.

Summary

In this chapter, we have done a lot of work to take our project and start to organize things a little better by organizing our Ansible playbooks into roles. We gave an overview of what roles are and how to use them, as well as discussed the directory structure and how everything is organized. We implemented a Django server as part of our deployment and used some extra functionality along the way by introducing conditional tasks, tags, and command-line variables.

In the next chapter, we will take our knowledge of roles further by introducing you to **Ansible Galaxy**, which is an online environment where you can search for roles created by the community that could be suitable for your work. We will take you on a journey on how you can work with the environment to search and install roles and also create your own to share with the rest of the world. Finally, we will give you some useful information on creating your own Ansible modules, as well as keeping our secret files and passwords safe.

## CHAPTER 4

Custom Ansible Modules, Vaults, and Galaxies

I think we've created a good base of Ansible knowledge in the previous chapters to now work further. This chapter will hopefully continue to allow your knowledge to grow. If we think about the previous chapters, they were more about creating a foundation to our work. This chapter will hopefully allow us to increase the speed in which we implement our projects as well as allow us to start to customize our projects faster.

Even though Ansible comes with such a huge amount of preinstalled modules, there may be the need to create your own module in some situations. Conversely, we have been creating our own roles, but in some circumstances, it may be easier to see if the Ansible community has created something which could fit your needs.

We are going to start our work in this chapter with a look at the standard way Ansible deals with secret information and passwords. We've been promising this for a while but will use the start of this chapter to give you the information you need to start using **Ansible Vault** in your project. The bulk of this chapter though will then take you through using **Ansible Galaxy** and creating your own modules to use in your projects.

This chapter will take you through some of the more advanced features of Ansible, and we will be using our project to help you introduce the following:

- We will start the chapter by looking at how we can use **Ansible Vault** to manage our project passwords and secret information.

- We will then introduce you to **Ansible Galaxy** and how you can start to work with and use prebuilt roles in your projects.

- We will take this further by showing you how to simplify your environment implementation by using Ansible Galaxy as a template to your future role creation.

- With the tools provided by Ansible, we will then take some time to show you how to add your own roles to the collaboration environment to allow other users to use your own roles.

- In the last part of the chapter, we will take a break from roles and demonstrate how you can create your own modules and how to use them in your projects.

So, without further delay, we'll get started with the chapter and get you comfortable with these new concepts.

Keeping Secrets with Ansible Vault

We have discussed in our previous chapters that keeping our passwords in plain text is not the best way to store them, and I promised we would address this. Luckily, Ansible has a way of encrypting our data to make sure it's secure by using the **ansible-vault** command. This will allow you to work with sensitive files using a password or password file to make sure your data is secure when being deployed to your environment.

As we've seen in our previous chapters, we have moved our variables into a designated var directory for each role. This is a perfect start for us as we can now use **ansible-vault** to encrypt the data and keep our password a secret.

We already have a good starting point to use ansible-vault with our current project, so log into your work environment and we will get started with using this feature in our project, specifically as part of our **db_server** role as this uses a clear text password for our MySQL database:

1. Our variable for our db_server role is currently in the **main.yml** file. We will start by moving this to a new file, specifically for our test environment. This will mean we can create a different variables file for any further environments we wish to then create, for example, a production environment, and will then use a different password:

```
mv roles/db_server/vars/main.yml roles/db_server/
vars/test_environment.yml
```

Note We need to make sure we move the file and rename it. If we leave a copy of the file as main.yml, Ansible will still use this file by default, and we will also have an unencrypted password left in our Ansible role.

---

2. We can now encrypt the data so it will be secure
    using a password and by using the **encrypt** option
    the **ansible-vault** command provides. Enter the
    following command and you will be prompted to
    enter your password directly into the command line:

**ansible-vault encrypt roles/db_server/vars/
test_environment.yml**

```
New Vault password:
Confirm New Vault password:
Encryption successful
```

3. If we have a look through our variables file, we will
    be able to see it is now encrypted, and we are not
    able to see the password we originally placed in the
    file. Use the head command as we have here to view
    the first five lines of the file:

head -n5 roles/db_server/vars/test_environment.yml

```
$ANSIBLE_VAULT;1.1;AES256
6664323731653433633736333336338636165633635353396463616
6656537363664626162306 1363
6439323661303736323137353323861363039353738333630
0a3933316366316634626235363539 3
3963343262336630643435306631633163323239646439633 23532
6230343634323336 43136 34656
343036373533383565
0a3534303964343864366234373238356162346333623133 353239
6662343
```

4. We can now use the **ansible-vault** command to
    make sure our data is still intact by using the **view**
    option with the file we just encrypted. Enter the

following ansible-vault command where you will be prompted again for the password you used to encrypt the file with:

ansible-vault view roles/db_server/vars/test_ environment.yml

```
Vault password:
---
mysql_root_password: password
```

As you can see, although our data is now encrypted, we are able to view it with this option and see the specific variables in the file.

5. Before we run our playbook again, we need to make sure the db_server role is able to use different environment variables when needed. Open the roles/db_server/tasks/main.yml file and add the following task to the top of the file:

```
1 ---
2 - name: load the variables for this environment
3   include_vars: "{{ env }}_environment.yml"
```

The role will now make sure all the variables in the specific environment are loaded before the rest of the tasks are run. We just need to specify the env name as part of our command line to make sure it is loaded correctly.

6. All we need to do now is run our playbook and use the new encrypted variables. We can do this by running our playbook command with the **--ask-vault-pass** option, which will then allow us to enter the password we specified earlier when we first

encrypted the file. We also use a second variable in the command line to make sure the correct environment is being used to load variables:

```
ansible-playbook -i hosts site.yml -e django_app_
location=`pwd` -e env=test --ask-vault-pass
```

```
Vault password:
```

We can also use a password file, which includes our password, so if we needed to run the playbook via an automated process, we simply make sure the password file is available when the playbook is run. This may seem a little insecure, but remember, you can ensure the security of the file and permissions to ensure the data is also kept safe. We can continue with our project and try this now.

7. When we use ansible-vault and reference a password file, we simply need to place the file in a directory accessible by the current user. In this instance, we will create a text file in our current directory. It's a little obvious, but we will call it **password_file.txt**:

```
touch password_file.txt
```

8. Now open the file with your text editor, and add in the same password you used to create the vault file earlier. Nothing else needs to be added to the file, simply the password in plain text. Save the file before proceeding.

9. We can now use this file to run our playbooks with the **--vault-password-file** option. To test it, we will use the view option of **ansible-vault** as we did

earlier to view our encrypted variables file. Run the
following command to view the encrypted variables
file, this time using a text file:

ansible-vault view roles/db_server/vars/test_
environment.yml --vault-password-file
password_file.txt

```
---

mysql_root_password: password
```

Here, we were able to now view the data in the
encrypted file without needing to type in our
password. If we were to run our playbook again,
we would use the same **--vault-password-file**
command option with **ansible-playbook**.

10. If we want to **edit** our encrypted file or make a
change to our encrypted data, we can use the edit
option with the **ansible-vault** command to open
the file and allow us to edit as if we were using a
text editor on the file directly. Run the following
command and you will be able to see we can now
edit the file as needed:

ansible-vault edit roles/db_server/vars/test_
environment.yml --vault-password-file
password_file.txt

11. If you wish to change the password you used to
encrypt the file with, you need to use the **rekey**
option. You do need to remember the original
password though before you can change it. Run the
following command to change the password used to

encrypt and decrypt the test_environment.yml file.
You should see a **"Rekey successful"** reply on the
command line if you are successful:

```
ansible-vault rekey roles/db_server/vars/test_
environment.yml --ask-vault-pass
```

```
Vault password:
New Vault password:
Confirm New Vault password:
Rekey successful
```

12. Finally, to decrypt the encrypted file, we use the
    decrypt option of the ansible-vault command.
    Run the following command, and if successful, you
    should now be able to open the **test_environment.
    yml** file as you normally would with your text editor:

```
ansible-vault decrypt roles/db_server/vars/test_
environment.yml --ask-vault-pass
```

We've come to the end of our discussion on using Ansible Vault in
your project. We have just scraped the surface of using the ansible-vault
command with our playbooks, but hopefully, this will give you enough
information to get you started and make sure you are keeping your secrets
safe. We will now move onto using and working with Ansible Galaxy as part
of our Ansible projects.

Note   This chapter contains a large number of command-line
commands. As with all the chapters in this book, there is a list of all
the command-line commands in the README file for the chapter in
the GitHub repository: `practical_ansible_ed2/README.md` at
`main · vincesesto/practical_ansible_ed2 · GitHub`.

Ansible Galaxy

Ansible Galaxy is a place where the Ansible community can share and reuse Ansible content. Considering the work you've done in previous chapters, why would you need this as we have become so proficient in creating and deploying our own roles? Sometimes, the unfortunate reality of our work is we simply don't have the time. This is where **Ansible Galaxy** can come in and fill the gap between the architecture of an environment and completing the work.

The best thing about galaxy is the content is packaged as **roles**, so this is a perfect progression from our previous chapter as we have been working extensively with roles and you hopefully understand how they work within our playbooks. By using galaxy, we can get started with our projects a lot faster as it allows us to search for roles made by the community and download and run them on your own environment.

This works both ways, as you can also share roles you've created with the rest of the community. By using your **GitHub** credentials, you can log into galaxy and share your content for others to use.

Even though we haven't been using them, we have had the tools to work with galaxy all along. The **ansible-galaxy** command comes standard with the application we installed at the start of this book. You can use the command to install roles, create roles, and perform tasks on the Ansible Galaxy website. Make note the ansible-galaxy command works directly with the galaxy website provided by Ansible.

Searching and Working with Ansible Galaxy Roles

To search through the Ansible Galaxy database to try and find a role we may need for our project, we can use the search parameter with the **ansible-galaxy** command. The search option allows us to not only specify a search term to look for, but we can also search for roles made by a particular user.

The following section will help us demonstrate how to use some basic ansible-galaxy commands, so feel free to work with us, so log back into your working environment to get started:

1. Even though we've created our own Django role in our previous chapter, we can start by having a look to see if there are any roles created and available in galaxy already. Run the following command that will use the **search** parameter with the **type** of role we are looking for:

    ansible-galaxy search django

    ```
    Found 30 roles matching your search:
    Name                        Description
    ----                        -----------
    ansible.django-gulp-nginx   Ansible Container
                                Django demo
    ansible.django-template     An Ansible Container
                                project template ansible.
                                nginx-container
    ansible-lab.pip             Pip (Python
                                Package Index)

    ...
    vforgione.uwsgi-emperor     A role for installing and
                                initializing
    vforgione.uwsgi-vassal      A role for installing
                                a Python
    Wtower.django-deploy        Deploy Django on Plesk
    Wtower.django-prepare       Prepare the launch of
                                a Django
    ```

We've restricted the number of entries we were provided from the search command as we had 30 roles provided and available which will hopefully set up a Django environment for you if you use them.

2. If you know the author of the role you were looking for, you could use the **--author** option as part of your search to only provide the roles in galaxy which have been authored by the author specified. Run the following command to search for a Django-specific role created by the account **ScorpionResponse**:

ansible-galaxy search django --author ScorpionResponse

```
Found 1 roles matching your search:
Name                      Description
----                      -----------
ScorpionResponse.django   Installer for a
                          Django project
```

3. If we wanted to then see if this author has created any other roles and has them stored in galaxy, we can exclude the role we want to search for and only leave the --author option. Run the following command to search for all roles created by the author ScorpionResponse:

ansible-galaxy search --author ScorpionResponse

```
Found 17 roles matching your search:
Name                      Description
----                      -----------
ScorpionResponse.celery   Installer for Celery
```

```
ScorpionResponse.django          Installer for a
                                 Django project
ScorpionResponse.git             Install Git
ScorpionResponse.gunicorn        Installer for gunicorn
ScorpionResponse.nginx           Installer for nginx
ScorpionResponse.nltk            Install NLTK and
                                 NLTK data
ScorpionResponse.personal_dev    Personal Development
                                 Configuration
ScorpionResponse.pip             Install Pip
ScorpionResponse.supervisord     Installer for
                                 supervisord
```

4. If we need some more information on a role we've found, we can then use the **info** option to provide us with the relative information on the role we want to hopefully install and use. Run the following command to gain further information on the ScorpionResponse.django we discussed earlier in this section of the chapter:

ansible-galaxy info ScorpionResponse.django

```
Role: ScorpionResponse.django
       description: Installer for a Django project
       active: True
       commit: 2bc72d5b2ed7c2eb652acc89bdde9f7b0
       9700182
       commit_message: allow git checkout to
       target specific version
       commit_url: https://github.com/
       ScorpionResponse
       ...
```

5. We can also check to see if we have any galaxy roles
    already installed on our system. We can use the
    list option with the ansible-galaxy command to
    see what galaxy roles are already installed on our
    system. Run the following command and we should
    see a zero result:

    ansible-galaxy list --roles-path roles/

    The list option will look in the default locations for
    your roles such as /etc/ansible/roles/; this is why we
    also use the --roles-path option to specify where we
    store roles on our system.

Note   To follow along with the next part of this exercise, you will
need to have a GitHub account, which will allow you to set up an
account on Ansible Galaxy. If you don't have an account already, you
will need to set one up in this URL: https://github.com/.

---

6. If we want to import, delete, or set up roles on
    Ansible Galaxy, you will need to have a galaxy
    account and be logged in. If you have not done it
    already, head to this website to create an account
    in Ansible Galaxy and you will be presented with a
    login screen like the image in Figure 4-1: **https://
    galaxy.ansible.com/login**.

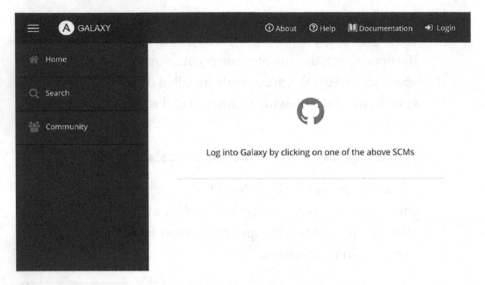

Figure 4-1. *The Ansible Galaxy Login Page*

> We will do some work later with the galaxy website,
> but for now, we will move back to the command line
> to show you how to log in once your account has
> been created.

7. Once our galaxy account has been created, we
   should now be able to log in through the command
   line by using the **login** option with our ansible-
   galaxy command. Run the following command to
   log in to your account:

ansible-galaxy login

```
We need your GitHub login to identify you.
This information will not be sent to Galaxy, only to
api.github.com.
The password will not be displayed.
```

```
Use --github-token if you do not want to enter your
password.
```

```
Github Username: vincesesto
Password for vincesesto:
Successfully logged into Galaxy as vincesesto
```

Recently, GitHub has introduced the use of
tokens for developers the ability to log in from the
command line. If you are having issues with the
command-line login, you may need to create a
token from the Develop Settings on GitHub and
using a command, similar to the following:

ansible-galaxy login --github-token
<token_provided_by_github>

8. We are now at the point where we can use the
    install option to install a role found in galaxy. To
    start, make sure you are back working on your test
    environment and make sure you are in the test_
    playbooks directory where we have been working
    with our current Ansible project:

9. Run the following ansible-galaxy command to
    install the **SimpliField.users** role from galaxy. We
    are also using the **--roles-path** option to specify
    where we are installing the role and adding it to our
    roles directory in our current working system:

**ansible-galaxy install SimpliField.users --roles-
path roles/**

```
- downloading role 'users', owned by SimpliField
- downloading role from https://github.com/SimpliField/
  ansible-users/archive/master.tar.gz
```

```
- extracting SimpliField.users to /test_playbook/roles/
  SimpliField.users
- SimpliField.users (master) was installed successfully
```

We can see from the preceding output the **SimpliField.users** role downloads and extracts into our roles directory.

10. Use the tree command from the command line as we have shown in the following to view the files in the roles/SimpliField.users directory. We can see the setup of the role is exactly the same as what we have been setting up manually as part of our own roles:

tree roles/SimpliField.users/
```
SimpliField.users/
├── meta
│   └── main.yml
├── README.md
├── tasks
│   └── main.yml
└── tests
        ├── inventory
        └── test.yml
3 directories, 5 files
```

11. To then use the role we have just installed from Ansible Galaxy, we need to create a playbook YAML file which will work directly using the role. Start by creating a new file called new_user.yml as we have here:

touch new_user.yml

12. Open the new_user.yml file with your text editor.
     Add in the following code which creates a new
     playbook using the new role. Line 4 shows the
     playbook is using the SimpliField.users role. Lines
     5–11 then set up the new user specifying the values
     needed to set up the new user account, including
     the name, comment, createhome, home, and shell
     details:

```
1  ---
2  - hosts: all
3    roles:
4    - role: SimpliField.users
5      users:
6      - simplifield:
7        name: "simplifield"
8        comment: "simplifield user"
9        createhome: "yes"
10       home: "/home/simplifield"
11       shell: "/bin/false"
```

13. We can now run this new playbook the same way we
     have been previously, and it will create the new user
     with username simplifield using the SimpliField.
     users role we installed from galaxy:

```
ansible-playbook -i hosts new_user.yml
PLAY [all] ****************************************
**********

TASK [Gathering Facts] ***************************
**********

ok: [localhost]
```

```
TASK [SimpliField.users : create user {{ item.name }}]
changed: [localhost] => (item={u'comment':
u'simplifield user', u'shell': u'/bin/fal\
se', u'name': u'simplifield', u'createhome': u'yes',
u'simplifield': None, u'home': \
u'/home/simplifield'})
PLAY RECAP *****************************************
***********
localhost                  :
ok=2    changed=1   unreachable=0   failed=0
```

14. If the preceding playbook executed successfully, the
    new user would now have been created, and we can
    verify it by looking through the /etc/password file on
    our system. Run the following command to look for
    the simplifield user we created in the previous step:

    cat /etc/passwd | grep simplifield

    ```
    simplifield:x:1003...user:/home/simplifield:/bin/false
    ```

15. Ansible-galaxy list.

16. We will be able to remove the role from the
    environment, so let's try removing the role we
    downloaded. Of course, we will be able to achieve
    this through the ansible-galaxy command by using
    the **remove** option. Run the following command
    which is very similar to the install command we ran
    previously:

    **ansible-galaxy remove SimpliField.users --roles-
    path roles/**

    ```
    - successfully removed SimpliField.users
    ```

Just as we did when we installed the role, we used the **--roles-path** option to specify where we installed the role to make sure the directories installed are cleaned up and removed.

We've covered off the basic ways to interact with Ansible Galaxy, but continue with the following section of this chapter to see how you can perform some of the more advanced ways to work with galaxy.

Downloading and Installing Multiple Roles from Galaxy

There may be a situation where you're needing to download numerous roles from galaxy. This can be simplified by providing a requirements file when we run our install command, instead of needing to run multiple install commands for each of the roles we need. The file we provided to the install command needs to be in YAML format, and although it only needs the **src** value specified, it can also include the **scm**, **version**, and **name**. Each option is detailed as follows:

- **src** – This is the source of the role. We've been using galaxy roles so far, and they have simply been in the format of **authorname.rolename**, but if it is from any other source, you'll need to specify the **URL** with a git extension to the role.

- **scm** – The only source code management ansiblegalaxy is able to use at the time of writing is either **git** or **hg** (Mercurial).

- **version** – This is the version you want to install and can also include the tag value or branch name you wish to use. Ansible will always default to use the **master** branch.

- **name** – You can also provide a name for the role to
  download. Some users might feel the names provided
  to galaxy may not be descriptive enough, so this option
  allows you to provide your own name to the role. It will
  default to the galaxy name if not specified.

With the previous work we did using Ansible Galaxy, the following
exercise will demonstrate how you can create a requirements file to install
your galaxy roles instead of performing manual commands. If you are not
logged into your development system, do this now so we can demonstrate
how to create a basic requirements file:

1. Our requirements file will be a YAML file, similar to
   most other configuration files and playbooks used
   by Ansible. Run the following command to create
   the requirements.yml file ready to be set up with our
   galaxy role:

```
touch requirements.yml
```

2. Open the requirements.yml file with your text editor
   and add in the following code. The details should
   be self-explanatory, but we can quickly note line 4
   provides the galaxy role as we would use with the
   install command. Line 6 provides an alternative
   name to be used when the role is downloaded. If we
   wanted to add further roles, we would simply add
   them to the file:

```
1 # File name requirements.yml
2
3 # Install from Ansible Galaxy
4 - src: SimpliField.users
5
6   name: supersecretrole
```

3. Save the file, but before we run the command on our system, we can export the path of our roles directory in our command line which Ansible will then make sure our requirements are installed in that directory:

export ANSIBLE_ROLES_PATH="roles"

4. Now run the following ansible-galaxy command which uses the install command and includes the -r option and the requirements.yml file:

ansible-galaxy install -r requirements.yml

```
- downloading role 'users', owned by SimpliField
- downloading role from https://github.com/
  SimpliField/ansible-users/archive/master.tar.gz
- extracting supersecretrole to /root/prac-ansible/
  chapter4/test_playbooks/roles/supersecretrole
- supersecretrole (master) was installed successfully
```

5. Perform a listing of the roles directory to make sure we have installed the role from the requirements. yml file correctly:

ls -l roles/supersecretrole

```
total 16
-rw-rw-r-- 1 root root  683 Aug 11  2016 README.md
drwxr-xr-x 2 root root 4096 Sep  8 16:21 meta
drwxr-xr-x 2 root root 4096 Sep  8 16:21 tasks
drwxr-xr-x 2 root root 4096 Sep  8 16:21 tests
```

We've worked quickly to get our requirements.yml file set up and working in our environment. Although you may not see the benefit of using this method, imagine if you had a large number of galaxy roles you needed to install on your system, you could simply list all of the roles in your requirements file to be installed all at once.

Moving Further with Ansible Galaxy

We've done a lot of work in our previous chapter to set up roles from scratch, as it was a perfect way to learn specifically what each part or directory in the role does. We can now take some time to show you how to use ansible-galaxy to speed things up as it will create all the relevant directories and base files needed to get you started with creating your own Ansible roles.

We can use a basic example to show how Ansible roles are created with the ansible-galaxy command, so log back into your working environment and we will get started with this example:

1. If we create our roles using the ansible-galaxy command, it will create the role in the directory we are working in. So, start by moving into the roles directory so we can be consistent with all the other roles we have created so far:

    cd roles/

    Unfortunately, the init option does not yet recognize the –roles-path option that we have been using so far.

2. The ansible-galaxy command has the **init** option available to create a new role in your project. Run the following command as we have to create a new role called **test_role**:

    ansible-galaxy init test_role
    ```
    test_role was created successfully
    ```

3. Our new role directory called test_role should have been created in your current directory. If we perform the tree command on this directory, we will be able to see all the relevant directories and default files created for us:

tree test_role/

```
test_role/
├── defaults
│   └── main.yml
├── files
├── handlers
│   └── main.yml
├── meta
│   └── main.yml
├── README.md
├── tasks
│   └── main.yml
├── templates
├── tests
│   ├── inventory
│   └── test.yml
└── vars
        └── main.yml
8 directories, 8 files
```

4. As we can see, all of our default files have been created in their relevant directories. Run the following command to see nothing except our three dashes (---) that are in the defaults/main.yml file:

cat test_role/defaults/main.yml

```
---
```

5. The cool thing about the init option is that it allows you to define your own **template** or **skeleton** of directories to be created when you initiate your new role. Let's say we wanted to create a set of directories and defaults for our role, just as we have in the test_ role but without the tests directory. Start by making our test_role look the way we want it to by removing the tests directory from it:

rm -rf test_role/tests/

6. We can now use the **--role-skeleton** option to show which role we want to use as our template to create our new role. Run the following command which specifies the test_role as our template for our new role:

ansible-galaxy init --role-skeleton=test_role test_skeleton_role
    test_skeleton_role was created successfully

7. If we perform a tree command on our new role, we will now be able to see it has used our new template and not created the tests directory:

tree test_skeleton_role/

```
test_skeleton_role/
├── defaults
│   └── main.yml
├── files
├── handlers
│   └── main.yml
├── meta
│   └── main.yml
```

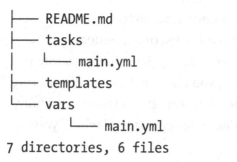

```
├── README.md
├── tasks
│   └── main.yml
├── templates
└── vars
        └── main.yml
7 directories, 6 files
```

This is a great way to define a set of standards for your own projects. If you have users that are new to Ansible, you could create a template for your projects and then get them to create any of their own roles using this template. There is still a lot more work for us to do with Ansible Galaxy, so keep moving with the next section of this chapter to demonstrate how we can start to contribute to Ansible Galaxy and import your roles into the web applications.

Contributing to Ansible Galaxy

Now we have our new roles created for our environment; what if we wanted to then share them to across the world by adding them to Ansible Galaxy? Well, this is also a straightforward process. There are one or two things you need to make sure of before you import your new role into galaxy:

- **Create accurate and usable documentation.** The **init** option of the ansible-galaxy command creates a **README.md** file with template ready for you to fill in and ensure that anyone who needs to use your role on galaxy has all the details available to do so as quickly as possible.

- **Give accurate metadata information.** A template is also created when you run init in the **meta/main.yml** file. It has a list of generic information that will allow your role to be classified and tagged by Ansible Galaxy.

129

- **Ensure you have dependencies listed**. The metadata also allows you to provide a list of dependencies your role needs to function correctly. If you create a role you want to add to galaxy, you may want to install your role on a blank system to make sure it will run successfully, as you may have a dependency installed which you didn't remember.

All that's then needed for anyone to import a role they have created as part of their project and add it to Ansible Galaxy. Once complete, all you need to do is log into galaxy and import the role from the interface. We can do this with one of our examples we have created in the previous section of this chapter. Log back into your working environment, and we will walk through the process:

1. Before we can import our **test_skeleton_role**, we need to make sure the README.md file and metadata have been updated. Open the **README. md** file with your text editor and add in the following details to allow users to know exactly what we are doing. Feel free to fill in the file with your own information if you wish:

```
1 Test Skeleton Role
2 =========
3 Testing how to add roles to Ansible Galaxy
4
5 Requirements
6 ------------
7 There are no requirements for the role.
8
9 Role Variables
10 --------------
```

```
11 There are no variables needed for the role.
12
13 Dependencies
14 ------------
15 There are no dependencies for the role.
16
17 Example Playbook
18 ----------------
19 The role does not have any example playbooks yet.
20
21 License
22 -------
23 BSD
24
25 Author Information
26 ------------------
27 Vincent Sesto
```

2. Save the README.md file and now open the **meta/main.yml** file that was created as part of the **test_skeleton_role** role. Open the file with your text editor to update the following details into the file. Add in the details for the first four lines which include the role description and if you like your company. The following details are what I used, but please use your own details:

```
1 galaxy_info:
2   author: vincesesto
3   description: This is a test role
4   company: No Company
```

3. All other details in the meta.yml file have default data available. You can leave the default values for this exercise, but move into line **42** and add in a sample tag as we have in the following entry:

42   galaxy_tags: [test_role]

4. There are a number of different ways you can import your role into Ansible Galaxy. If you are already using GitHub to store your code, this is one of the easier ways and the way we will proceed. Save your meta.yml file you have been working on and continue on.

Note   If you have not used git before, creating and committing your work to GitHub is a straightforward process. You will first need to create a repository on the GitHub website, where you will be provided with a repository domain. Once you have this domain, you simply need to return to the command line, initialize the repository, add and commit the repository, and then push the changes to GitHub with the following commands:

git init – To initialize your code.

git add . – To select all the code to be added.

git commit -m "First Commit" – To commit the changes ready to push.

git remote add origin <repository_domain> – So git knows where the repository is located.

git push -u origin master – To push the changes to your repository.

Your changes should now be available on GitHub to be added to Ansible Galaxy.

---

5. Once you have your repository added to GitHub,
    access the Ansible Galaxy website and make sure
    you are logged into your account.

6. Once logged in, select "My Content" from the
    left menu or go to the domain **https://galaxy.
    ansible.com/my-content/namespaces**.

7. Click the **Add Content** button and you will be
    presented with the following options, as we have
    shown in Figure 4-2, to **Import Role from GitHub**,
    which we will use, or **Upload New Collection**,
    which can import from your systems hard drive.

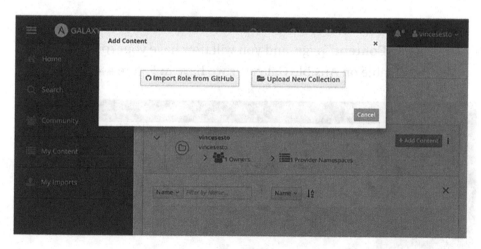

Figure 4-2. *Importing Content from Your GitHub Account*

8. Ansible Galaxy will connect to your GitHub account
    and will allow you to select the repository that
    includes your role. Select the repository you wish to
    add from GitHub as we have in Figure 4-3.

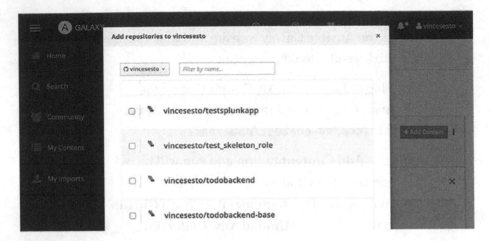

Figure 4-3. *Importing Content from Your GitHub Account*

9.   Click Save and you should then be taken back to the
     "My Content" page, and you will now have your role
     available on Ansible Galaxy as we have in Figure 4-4.

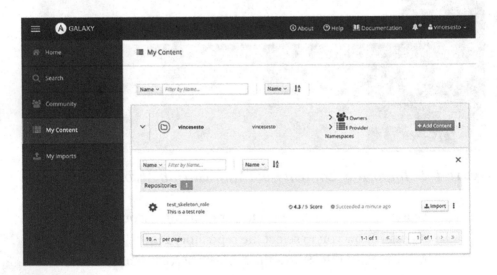

Figure 4-4. *The My Content Page with New Role Added*

10. Click the link for our new **test_skeleton_role**, and you should now be presented with an image similar to Figure 4-5. We now have all our details available from our README.md and meta.yml file we set up previously for others to search and use.

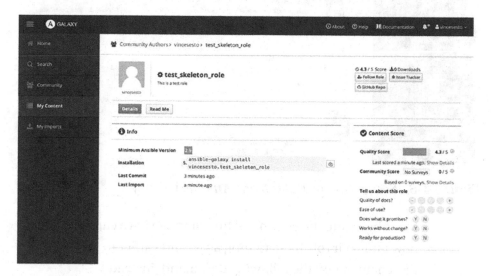

Figure 4-5. *Viewing Your Roles from Ansible Galaxy*

11. We searched for roles from the command line earlier in this chapter. We can see how this works on the web interface by clicking the **Search** option on the menu. Click the Search option from the left menu, and enter **test_skeleton_role** into the text box at the top of the screen as we have in Figure 4-6, and see if we find the role you have just created.

Figure 4-6. *Searching for Roles from Ansible Galaxy*

12. Move back into the command line, and see if we can
     now find your role by searching as we did earlier in
     this chapter. Run the following command, instead
     using your galaxy account name to make sure your
     new role is provided as a result:

     ansible-galaxy search --author vincesesto

     ```
     Found 1 roles matching your search:
       Name                           Description
       ----                           -----------
       vincesesto.test_skeleton_role   This is a test role
     ```

13. If you want to now delete the role from Ansible
     Galaxy, this can be done from the web interface or
     from the command line with the following command:

     ansible-galaxy remove vincesesto.test_skeleton_role

By now, I am sure we've provided you with enough information for you to work with the community to collaborate, improve, and speed up your work by using Ansible Galaxy. Hopefully, you can see the benefit and will be able to make use of roles other users in the community have generated to speed up your project work. This is the end of the work we will be doing with Ansible Galaxy, with the final part of this chapter dedicated to showing you how you can create your own Ansible modules.

Building Your Own Ansible Modules

We've seen that Ansible provides us with a huge amount of modules, and it almost seems we would never need to create our own Ansible module. But as new technology is introduced and as we may have "In House" applications which are not supported by a wider community, this may come up at some point. As you have seen so far, Ansible provides a way to do so much, and creating your own module is no different. All you need to know is a little bit of Python or can script in the Linux shell to get you started.

Ansible modules can be written in any language you really want; most of the modules you'll see are written in either Python or Linux shell. In the following exercises, we will create a simple module in Python and then create something a little more involved using the Linux shell.

As with most programming exercises, it's customary to produce a **"Hello World"** example to show how everything works. We will be creating the new module with **Python**, but don't worry, we're specifically keeping it basic for now in case you are not familiar with the language, and we can talk you through it. So let's get stuck in straight away to show you how creating your own modules will work:

1. Access your development environment, and from within your main working directory, we need somewhere to hold our new modules. Run the following command to create a directory called **library** where we will store our new module:

    ```
    mkdir library
    ```

Note   We have created the directory for our modules in our current working directory, meaning it will be available to any of our playbooks we wish to create and run from this directory. If we wanted to create a module that was specifically made for one of our roles, we would need to create a library directory as part of our role directory structure.

---

2. Create a new file called **hello_module.py** in the library directory by running the following command:

    ```
    touch library/hello_module.py
    ```

3. Open the **library/hello_module.py** file you just created with your text editor, and enter in the following Python code:

    ```
    1 #!/usr/bin/python
    2
    3 from ansible.module_utils.basic import *
    4
    ```

```
5 def main():
6         module = AnsibleModule(argument_spec={})
7         response = {"hello": "world!"}
8         module.exit_json(changed=False, meta=response)
9
10 if __name__ == "__main__":
11        main()
```

If you are not familiar with Python, we can give you a quick rundown of the code in the file. Line 1 needs to be specified to allow the script to run with the locally installed version of Python. Line 3 then imports the modules which will let it run with Ansible. Lines 5–8 provide the function that is going to run when we run the module; specifically, line 6 provides the **AnsibleModule** class which allows us to handle incoming parameters and allows us to exit the program. Finally, lines 10 and 11 run the function when we run the module.

4. We can now create a playbook to run our new module. Create the file named newmodule_test. yml in your working directory with the following command:

touch newmodule_test.yml

5. Open the newmodule_test.yml file with your text editor, and enter the following details that will run the new module for us. The following playbook has lines 3–5 running the new module as a task, line 6

capturing the result as a variable named result, and
then line 7 outputting the result for us to display as
part of the playbook output:

```
1 ---
2 - hosts: localhost
3   tasks:
4   - name: testing our new module
5     hello_module:
6     register: result
7   - debug: var=result
```

6. All we need to do now is run the playbook to make
   sure it works. Run the following **ansible-playbook**
   command to run the newmodule_test.yml playbook
   and hopefully use our new modules successfully:

```
ansible-playbook -i hosts newmodule_test.yml

PLAY [localhost] ******************************
*********
TASK [Gathering Facts] ***********************
*********
ok: [localhost]
TASK [testing our new module]
***************************
ok: [localhost]
TASK [debug] *********************************
*********
ok: [localhost] => {
    "result": {
        "changed": false,
        "failed": false,
```

```
    "meta": {
        "hello": "world!"
    }
} }
PLAY RECAP ************************************
*********
localhost:
ok=3    changed=0    unreachable=0    failed=0
```

7. If all has gone well and we have not made any
    mistakes with our code, the playbook should run
    and output the desired **"Hello World"**.

    Creating our module in Python, specifically using
    the **ansible.module_utils.basic** Python library,
    simplifies things a little for us and ensures we
    are returning a JSON output for our code. This is
    really all we need to remember when creating our
    modules, and creating them as a Linux shell script
    will help us demonstrate this further.

8. We already have a library directory created for the
    modules we are creating. We can also place our
    Linux shell module in this directory. To create our
    new module, start by creating the new module
    named os_type.sh as we have with the following
    command:

    touch library/os_type.sh

9. Open the **os_type.sh** file with your text editor
    ready to create a basic module which will print the
    type of operating system the playbook is currently
    running on.

10. The code is going to be very simple. Add in the following code which simply runs the uname command on line 3 and adds the value into a variable named OS. We then provide our output as JSON format where we set the changed variable to false as we are only displaying values to the screen and then providing a value to the operating_system variable:

```
1 #!/bin/bash
2
3 OS="$(uname)"
4
5 echo "{\"changed\":false,\"operating_
  system\":\"$OS\"}"
```

11. Save the new module and open our newmodule_test.yml playbook we created earlier in this exercise, and with your text editor, change the module being used to now look like the following code where line 5 is now changed to use the new module called os_type:

```
1 ---
2 - hosts: localhost
3   tasks:
4   - name: testing our new module
5     os_type:
6     register: result
7   - debug: var=result
```

12. We can now run our new module. Use the command we have run in the following to run the os_type module as part of the playbook, and you should hopefully get a similar output as we have:

```
ansible-playbook -i hosts newmodule_test.yml

PLAY [localhost] ***********************************
TASK [Gathering Facts] *****************************
ok: [localhost]
TASK [testing our new module] *********************
ok: [localhost]
TASK [debug] **************************************
ok: [localhost] => {
    "result": {
        "changed": false,
        "failed": false,
        "operating_system": "Linux"
    }
}
PLAY RECAP ****************************************
localhost: ok=3   changed=0   unreachable=0   failed=0
```

We've highlighted the output of our running playbook to show the specific results of the os_type module. These results reflect directly with the output we see at the bottom of our output when our playbook completes. Although we have created a simple module, we could make things more advanced and set our output to change depending on specific conditions within the module.

For now, I hope we have been able to quickly demonstrate how you can create your own modules to run across your own playbooks if needed. This brings us to the end of this section of the chapter and also the end of this chapter.

Summary

This chapter has taken on a large scope of work. We started off this chapter with a look at how we can use **ansible-vault** to encrypt our sensitive data while deploying our playbooks. We then moved on to the bulk of this chapter which centered around **Ansible Galaxy** and working with the website and making use of the **ansible-galaxy** command. We learned how to search for roles, get more information, and install and remove roles. We then took some time to show you how you can contribute directly to the community and import your own roles into Ansible Galaxy.

We then used the remainder of the chapter to show you how you can create your own Ansible modules and use them within your deployments. Our next chapter will take you into the **Amazon Web Services Cloud**, showing you how you can use Ansible to deploy your environments directly into AWS. When we start working in the cloud, we will also start afresh with our next project, so don't stop now; you're making great progress.

## CHAPTER 5

Working with Ansible in the Amazon Cloud

I like to think we have taken you on a bell-shaped learning progression and we have covered a majority of the more difficult work you may be faced with when starting to learn Ansible. This foundation should allow us to power through the remainder of the chapters, showing you some more interesting features in Ansible to hopefully extend your knowledge further and introduce you to some features which will make your life and configuration management processes easier.

This chapter and the following chapters are going to take what you know already and then move it into the **Amazon Cloud**. We will be using quite a few of the skills learned from the previous chapters and combining them with specific modules and tools used to work with **Amazon Web Services (AWS)**.

In this chapter, we will work through the following:

- We will start with a quick discussion on AWS and why we have chosen to use this platform, and if needed, we will point you in the direction of some resources to help you get started.

- We will then start with the basic Ansible modules that work directly with **AWS** and get you started with deploying into your own AWS account.

© Vincent Sesto 2022

V. Sesto, *Practical Ansible*, https://doi.org/10.1007/978-1-4842-8643-2_5

- Our work will then turn to our next project where we will set out what we need to achieve and start to put our first cloud deployment in place using Ansible.

- We will then introduce how Ansible will install our **Splunk** application by the use of **user data** scripts.

- Finally, we will have a discussion on how you can pinpoint errors and where to start troubleshooting when your AWS cloud deployments go wrong.

Even though we're going to be working in AWS, we will be taking things slowly, so hopefully, if your experience is limited, you won't get lost with the work we are doing. You don't need to be proficient in AWS, and if you are, it will simply speed your progress through these following chapters. As we move through the different services and modules we use, we will make sure we give a brief description of the AWS work we are doing as we go.

So Why Amazon Web Services?

If you haven't used AWS before, you'll notice they provide infrastructure and IT services similar to the way a utility provides power and hot water. You don't pay any additional costs to how the infrastructure was purchased and licensed, and once you are no longer using these services, you turn it off and are no longer paying for it.

Even though there are a number of major players in the market including **Azure** (Microsoft), **Google Cloud**, **IBM Cloud**, and **Oracle**, at the time of writing, AWS was still the major player in the space. If you are using one of the other major platforms for your cloud services, there most likely will be Ansible modules created to work with and integrate with them.

AWS Is Not Free

Amazon Web Services is not free, but we will do our best to keep any costs low. Even though we will be trying our best to stick to the free tier, AWS offers a pay-as-you-go approach to the pricing of its cloud services. This is part of its mass appeal as companies across the world have utilized AWS to help reduce the cost of their infrastructure.

AWS Pricing

If you're interested in using AWS for your project and before you move further on with this chapter, the following link will provide you with more details on their pricing and how they calculate service rates: `https://aws.amazon.com/pricing/services/`.

Gaining Access to AWS

If you are already familiar with AWS, feel free to skip over this section as we are going to discuss some of the basics of AWS with regard to allowing Ansible the ability to interface with the application and make changes when needed.

If you haven't already set up your access to AWS, you will need to do this first as you will then have a **username** and **password**. This will most likely be for the root user, so it is wise to create a new user who can work as an administrator across your AWS account without having full root privileges.

If you are completely new to AWS and you need to set up a new account, you can do so by going to the following link:

`https://portal.aws.amazon.com/billing/signup#/start`

AWS Is Not Free   I just want to say this one more time as I don't want people to think there are no costs involved when services are run in AWS. As I said earlier, we will do our best to use free tier services, but the pricing model from Amazon could change since the writing of this book, so make sure you understand the pricing implemented by AWS.

If you are interested in finding out how to manage your AWS bill and even set up alarms to make sure you do not exceed a specific cost, please look at the following documentation on the subject:

```
https://docs.aws.amazon.com/awsaccountbilling/
latest/aboutv2/awsaccountbilling-aboutv2.pdf
```

You should now have an account with AWS and be able to access the console from a web browser. We will take a moment to walk through the process of setting up a new user on your account that will allow Ansible to interact with your AWS account:

1. Once logged in to the AWS web console, click the **Services** menu at the top left of the screen. When you are able to type into the search box, enter IAM, and when presented with an option to move to **IAM**, select it. This is how AWS manages users and identity and where we will set up a new user. Alternatively, you can go directly to the following URL as well: `https://console.aws.amazon.com/iam/home`

2. On the left side of the IAM web console, click the **Users** option, and then click the **Add user** button.

3. When adding a new user, you first see a screen
    similar to Figure 5-1, which allows you to enter a
    username and other details for the user. Enter a
    username familiar to you, and for now, select the
    AWS Management Console access check box. If
    you wish to set a password for the user at this point,
    feel free to do that, but you can always allow AWS
    to generate a password for you. If you leave the
    Require password reset check box as checked, you
    will need to log in as the new user before you can
    start using the account. Once you are happy with
    your selection, click the **Next: Permissions** button.

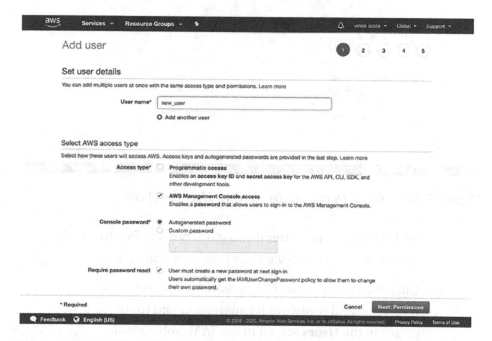

Figure 5-1. *Adding in Basic Details for Your AWS Administrator User*

4. You will now be presented with a screen similar
    to the one displayed in Figure 5-2, allowing you to
    add permissions to your new user. For now, click
    AdministratorAccess as we have in Figure 5-2 and
    then click the Next: Tags button to proceed.

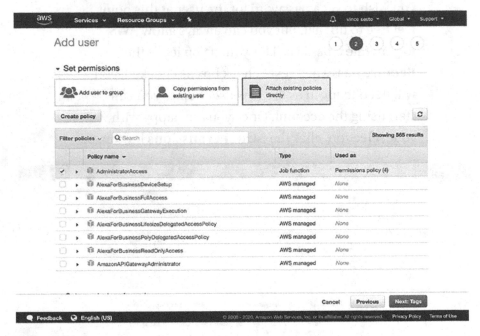

Figure 5-2. *Adding Permissions to New Users in AWS*

5. Add Tags to the new user if you wish, but feel free to
    leave it blank. Then review the new user and create.

6. Once the new user has been created, note the
    username and password if you need to and then
    return to the **Users** screen in the **IAM** web console.

7. Select the user you just created, as this will be the
    user which Ansible will interface with AWS. You
    should see a screen similar to Figure 5-3 showing

details of the new user we created. As you can see, this account has the **_AdministratorAccess_** policy attached to it to allow it to perform the tasks that we need to over the next chapter.

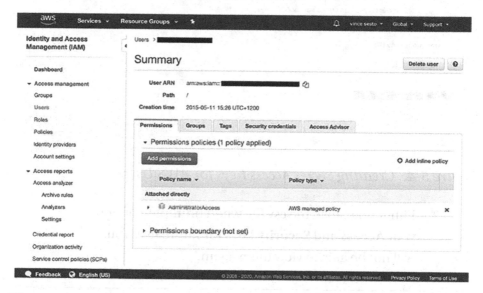

Figure 5-3. *Adding Permissions to New Users in AWS*

Note   You can see we have redacted some of the information in the image; this is so we can ensure the security of the account we are performing the work on.

8. Click the **_Security Credentials_** tab and then click the **_Create access key_** button. This will create a new access key for you to then use when running your Ansible playbooks. You will be presented with a success message like the one in Figure 5-4.

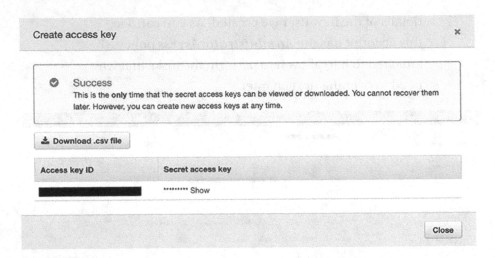

Figure 5-4. *Creating Secret Access Keys for AWS Users*

9. Either download the csv file when prompted or note
    your **Access** and **Security keys** for future use. You
    will not be able to view them again.

Note   AWS access keys are a major security risk. These keys need
to be kept private and secure at all times, and if someone gets hold
of an available access key, it could compromise the security of your
AWS account.

Make sure you never show anyone your keys, as well as ensuring you
never publish your keys to a public website or repository. Malicious
hackers will be able to gain access to your account and misuse it.
Please be careful.

---

10. To help us test if we are able to connect to AWS using our new user account keys, we can install the **awscli** application on our system. We will use the **pip3** command to install the package the same way we installed Ansible in our earlier chapters. Move back into your development environment and enter the following command into the command line:

```
pip3 install awscli
```

11. We can now set up our credentials to use the AWS access keys we just created. We can start by adding an **aws** directory in our home environment:

```
mkdir -pv ~/.aws
```

12. Now create a credentials file where we can store our access keys:

```
touch ~/.aws/credentials
```

13. Open the credentials file with your text editor and add in your user credentials. As I am working in Australia and New Zealand, I will be using the **ap-southeast2** region, but make sure you use the region which suits your needs:

```
1 [default]
2 aws_access_key_id = YOUR-ACCESS-KEY-HERE
3 aws_secret_access_key = YOUR-SECRET-ACCESS-KEY-HERE
4 region: YOUR-PREFERRED-REGION
```

14. We can now test access on the command line before we start to use Ansible. We can test to verify all our credentials are correct and we have access to our

environment. So make sure you are in your working environment and run the following command to use the Secure Token Service (sts) to verify the identity of the current user:

```
aws sts get-caller-identity
{
    "UserId": "YOUR-ACCESS-KEY-HERE",
    "Account": "ACCOUNT-NUMBER",
    "Arn": "arn:aws:iam::ACCOUNT-NUMBER:user/newuser"
}
```

If you have entered everything correctly, you should see something similar to the preceding output. We are basically making a call to AWS to find out the details of the credentials we have input. The output you would see would reflect your account and the username that owns the access keys you created.

Using Environment Variables to Access AWS

This is a quick section to let you know you don't need to always add your credentials on the host you are working with. You may be working on a temporary machine to perform a deployment and need to access AWS. You can instead add your credentials to the hosts **environment variables** to allow you to perform your Ansible work.

We can do exactly the same thing we did in the previous section by running the following command from the command line:

```
export AWS_ACCESS_KEY_ID=YOUR-ACCESS-KEY-HERE
export AWS_SECRET_ACCESS_KEY=YOUR-SECRET-ACCESS-KEY-HERE
export AWS_DEFAULT_REGION=YOUR-PREFERRED-REGION
```

This allows you to work as if you were on your work environment and run the same commands. When you log out, the environment variables will then be removed as well.

Ansible AWS Modules to Implement Our New Project

From what you've seen so far in this book, a lot of the functionality of Ansible relies on the modules you use when implementing your environment or configuration changes. This is no different from working with AWS. As there are such a large number of services available in AWS, we thought it would be a good idea to allow a couple of chapters to work through some of the more common services available. We also thought it would be a good time to introduce our new project.

Our New Splunk Implementation Project

As we discussed in the first chapter of this book, our second project will be a Splunk installation on AWS cloud infrastructure. In the following pages, we will start to set up the host that will house our new service as well. We will use Ansible to deploy Splunk and with temporary licenses onto the host.

This should get us to a usable state where we will then start to work further by adding a Splunk App onto the server. Our next chapter will then extend the environment further, but for now, we will get started with some of the basics and build upon our existing knowledge.

Note   With the modules you will be using in the following chapter, they all require the dependency of **boto** for Python3. As we have a running version of **awscli** installed on our system, you should not need to worry about this, but if you do see errors when running commands, this may be the first thing you can check.

One of the first places to start would be to create a basic virtual server instance within AWS under their **EC2 Service**. There is one thing we would need to do before creating our instance, and that would be to create a keypair to then allow us to **SSH** onto the server.

Let's log back into our work environment so we can get started:

1.   We are starting a new project, so run the following command to start by creating a new directory for us to work in and move into that directory:

     mkdir splunk_server; cd splunk_server

2.   We can start by creating a new **hosts** file, just like we did in our earlier chapters. As you can remember, these are the details of our servers we want to deploy changes to, so create the file with the following command:

     touch hosts

3.   We won't be deploying changes to a specific server, but instead, we will be interfacing with **AWS** to make our configuration changes. This means we only need to add in our **localhost** entry into our hosts file. Using your text editor, open the new hosts file to enter the following two lines:

     1 [local]
     2 localhost

4. There are two ways in which we can create our
    keypair to connect with our new server: either
    importing a file into the AWS console or creating a
    new one. In this exercise, we will use a small Ansible
    playbook to create a new keypair for our project.

5. Run the following command to create a new
    playbook called **create_key_pair.yml** which will
    perform the keypair creation for us:

touch create_key_pair.yml

6. Open the new playbook with your text editor and we
    can start to create our tasks. We only have one host
    in our hosts file, so this is now specified as **local** at
    the start of our playbook, which will work directly
    with AWS. Lines 6–9 then set up our first task using
    the **ec2_key** module to create a new key with the
    name and region specified. Line 10 then collects the
    output of this task and places it in a variable named
    ec2_key_result:

```
 1 ---
 2 - hosts: local
 3   connection: local
 4   gather_facts: no
 5   tasks:
 6   - name: Create a new EC2 key
 7     ec2_key:
 8       name: ansible-answers-key
 9       region: ap-southeast-2
10     register: ec2_key_result
11
```

7. Move down the playbook and enter the next task which will use the output from the previous tasks and place the private key details into a file ready for us to use. The task uses the **copy** module to get the contents of the variable we registered earlier, extract the **private_key** value, and place it in a new file called **splunkserver.pem** ready for us to use:

```
12   - name: Save private key
13     copy:
14         content: "{{ ec2_key_result.key.
           private_key }}"
15         dest: "./splunkserver.pem"
16         mode: 0600
17     when: ec2_key_result.changed
```

8. Although it's just a small playbook, it will give us an example of how we can start to interface and work with AWS. Save the playbook and then use the following command to run the playbook from the command line:

```
ansible-playbook -i hosts create_key_pair.yml
```

9. If the playbook ran successfully, we should be able to see both a splunkserver.pem file in our current working directory and the new key generated in the AWS console. Start by verifying our splunkserver. pem file has been generated with the following command, and you should see a similar output to the one we have, with the head command providing the first five lines of the file:

```
head -n 5 splunkserver.pem
-----BEGIN RSA PRIVATE KEY-----
MIIEpQIBAAKCAQEAuV6LADnQ3+mOrTcc2gwqlx/
QjVyp96KVCwQ92aStDb/YsZCOtP7QrteqoyTx
nzTuncp7rqgM3e1n6LTxy+5PKqxWIP9Gw16hUz8LFu+/
oTmKfegUqjdPLuPcZIld3koZ4q21YIuK
Fu2BgdRpgThVlS5yo9+ZNE6CWbNXJa7OamvI1ZLptWLQvYvt9pP65W
gadOkI 3QwEOQlEshj6moQj
RHovlyXtzxZhCblxN4rZzEF8tqrN86ftw71/
qpIhUR3GoU8r2DmIWx//kFBVDbM1eOOZ8iTSz66P
```

10. We can now see if the new key has been created on our AWS account. Log into our AWS console, click the Services drop-down menu at the top left of the screen, and select **EC2**. Select **Key pairs** from the left side of the screen, and you should now see your **ansible-answers-key** created in the console, as we can see in Figure 5-5.

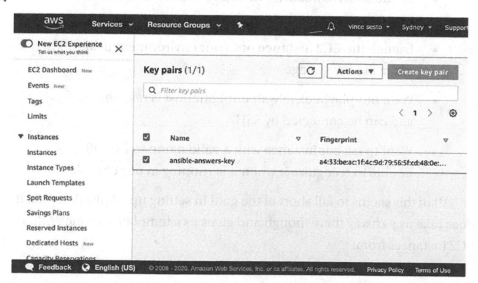

Figure 5-5. *Creating SSH Keypairs in Ansible and AWS*

As you can see, working with Amazon Web Services is very similar to the work we have performed so far in our previous chapters. Now we have a SSH keypair available to connect with any future servers we created; continue on with the following section of this chapter to start setting up our EC2 instance.

Creating Our AWS Instance

We could create our instance from the command line just like we've created our keypair, but as we learned in previous chapters, creating a role that is then used by a playbook is probably the best option for us in this instance as there would be a lot of different commands we would need to perform to get the job done.

If we mapped out what we need to provision a basic server, we will have to

- Create an **AWS Security Group** to control who can and who cannot access the server

- Launch the **EC2 instance** onto our environment using a specific AWS image

- Want our playbook to wait until our host is responsive and can be contacted by SSH

- Want to tag our instance with a valid name so we will be able to recognize it when it is running in our console

All of this seems to fall short of the goal in setting up a Splunk server. It does take us partway there though and gives us a template to create other EC2 instances from.

If you have logged out of your work environment, log back in so we can get back to work:

1. Start by creating a directory to store our new role in with the following mkdir command and then move into the directory after it is created:

mkdir roles; cd roles

2. Our last chapter demonstrated how we can set up our role by using the ansible-galaxy **init** command. Run the following command to create the necessary files for our new role which will be called **splunk_ server** and will be placed in our new directory called roles:

ansible-galaxy init splunk_server
```
- splunk_server was created successfully
```

3. If we perform a **tree** command on the roles directory, we will see our directories have been set up for us as part of the init command:

tree splunk_server/

```
splunk_server/
|-- README.md
|-- defaults
|    `-- main.yml
|-- files
|-- handlers
|    `-- main.yml
|-- meta
|    `-- main.yml
```

```
|-- tasks
|    `-- main.yml
|-- templates
|-- tests
|    |-- inventory
|    `-- test.yml
`-- vars
     `-- main.yml
8 directories, 8 files
```

4. With our role structure created, we can move
    directly into setting up our tasks. Start by opening
    the **splunk_server/tasks/main.yml** file and start by
    defining the security group for our new server. Line
    1 starts our YAML file, and we then move to defining
    our new task to create the security group using the
    ec2_group Ansible module. Lines 4, 5, and 6 provide
    the new security group with a name, description,
    and the region we want it set up in:

```
1 ---
2 - name: create the host security group
3   ec2_group:
4     name: "{{ ec2_sg_name }}"
5     description: security group for new host
6     region: "{{ ec2_region }}"
```

5. Continue to add details of the security group
    with the following lines of code, where we specify
    our inbound and outbound rules across lines 7
    through to 23:

```
 7    rules:
 8      - proto: tcp
 9        from_port: 22
10        to_port: 22
11        cidr_ip: 0.0.0.0/0
12      - proto: tcp
13        from_port: 8000
14        to_port: 8000
15        cidr_ip: 0.0.0.0/0
16      - proto: tcp
17        from_port: 443
18        to_port: 443
19        cidr_ip: 0.0.0.0/0
20    rules_egress:
21      - proto: all
22        cidr_ip: 0.0.0.0/0
23   register: basic_firewall
24
```

6. With our security group created, we can now use the
   ec2 Ansible module to create our server instance.
   Enter the following lines of code into your tasks file:

```
25 - name: launch the new ec2 instance
26   ec2:
27     group: "{{ ec2_sg_name }}"
28     instance_type: "{{ ec2_instance_type }}"
29     image: "{{ ec2_image }}"
30     wait: true
31     region: "{{ ec2_region }}"
32     keypair: "{{ ec2_keypair }}"
33     count: 1
34   register: ec2
```

The module needs a lot of arguments to complete the process. The **group** value is the security group we created earlier, the **instance_type** is the size of the AWS instance, the **image** is the AWS image we will be using, and the **keypair** is the SSH key we have defined earlier in our chapter. All of these values will be listed in our **variables** file. We will go into a little more detail on what each of these variables is when we define them.

7.   We have enough in our tasks file to simply launch our instance, but we should make sure the server is up and running before we make any other changes to the host. There are many times when we simply can't make any changes until it is accessible, so add in the following code to create a task that will wait for **port 22** to be accessible on the host and SSH to be available:

```
36 - name: wait for SSH to come up
37   wait_for:
38     host: '{{ item.public_ip }}'
39     port: 22
40     state: started
41   with_items: '{{ ec2.instances }}'
42
```

You'll notice we have more variables specified here. In this case, they are not needed to be specified as part of our code. Instead, these are defined by AWS when the items are created in the previous tasks. As an example, line 34 of the role registers the values created in the ec2 instance. These values are then used when we use the **with_items** function which is similar to a loop, but in this case, we only have one item in place, the **ec2** instance created by the code.

8. Lastly, we will need to set up **tags** for our instance so we will be able to recognize it when it comes up in our AWS console. If we don't, it will not have a name and only be recognized by the randomly generated AWS instance Id. Here, we use the **ec2_tag** module and set the **Name** tag to **splunkserver**:

```
43 - name: add a tag to the instance
44   ec2_tag:
45     resource: '{{ item.id }}'
46     region: '{{ ec2_region }}'
47     state: present
48   with_items: '{{ ec2.instances }}'
49   args:
50     tags:
51       Name: splunkserver
```

9. We now have all the tasks needed to set up the basics of our server instance. Save the file and we can then move on to completing the rest of the role.

10. There are a number of variables our tasks rely on, so this is a good time to set up our variables file. Open the roles/splunk_server/vars/main.yml file with your text editor and add in the following variable details:

```
1 ---
2 ec2_sg_name: "AnsibleSecurityGroup"
3 ec2_region: "ap-southeast-2"
```

```
4 ec2_instance_type: "t2.micro"
5 ec2_image: "ami-0d6fb2916ee0ab9fe"
6 ec2_keypair: "ansible-answers-key"
```

Even though there are only six lines here, there is a
lot to explain if you haven't worked with AWS before:

a. Line 2 is the **security group** name we set up in our
    tasks. You define security groups in AWS to provide
    access to services where needed.

b. We define the region of **ap-southeast-2** in line 3 as
    it will simply be placed in the default region if not
    specified. Make sure you are specifying a region you
    are comfortable with.

c. In line 4, we state the instance type, which is the size
    and specifications of the server we are deploying. The
    t2.micro is a small machine and should still be in the
    free pricing tier, but be able to do the work we need in
    this chapter.

d. We will discuss more about ec2 images, but for now,
    just note we have decided to use an up-to-date host
    running of **Amazon Linux** and once again in the
    free tier.

e. Lastly, line 6 is the **keypair** that we created earlier in
    this chapter.

11. We have made most of the changes to our role to
     start testing it out. Move back into the roles directory
     to finish up our playbook:

```
cd ../
```

12. We are almost at a point where we can deploy our server; first, we need to create a playbook to run the new role we have just created. Run the following command to create the file called **server_deploy. yml** in your working directory:

```
touch server_deploy.yml
```

13. Open the server_deploy.yml file with your text editor and add the finishing code to our playbook. As you know by now, the role we created does a bulk of the work, so our playbook will not be too involved:

```
1 ---
2 - hosts: localhost
3   connection: local
4   gather_facts: false
5   user: root
6   roles:
7     - splunk_server
```

As we are now using AWS and we have set up our connection, lines 2 and 3 are specifying we are running our deployment from our local machine. Line 4 tells Ansible it doesn't need to go around and gather information on our environment before deploying, and then lines 6 and 7 run our **Splunk server** role.

14. We can now deploy our server using our new
     splunk_server role. Run the following **ansible-
     playbook** command to deploy our new server:

ansible-playbook -i hosts server_deploy.yml

```
PLAY [local] *****************************************
TASK [Create the host security group] ****************
ok: [localhost]
TASK [Launch the new EC2 Instance] *******************
changed: [localhost]
TASK [Wait for SSH to come up] ***********************
ok: [localhost] => (item={u'kernel': None, u'root_
device_type': u'ebs',
...
TASK [Add tag to Instance(s)] ************************
changed: [localhost] => (item={u'kernel': None, u'root_
device_type': u'ebs',
...
PLAY RECAP *******************************************
localhost:
ok=4    changed=2    unreachable=0    failed=0
```

If all has gone well, you should see output similar
to the preceding one. Make note it will take a
number of minutes to complete as a server is being
provisioned by AWS.

15. Once the playbook has completed running, you
     should be able to log on to AWS, and from within the
     EC2 console, if you click the Instance menu on the
     left of the screen, you will see your deployed server

and hopefully one labeled as **"splunkserver"** and
ready to be accessed. You should see something
similar to Figure 5-6, showing the details of our
new server.

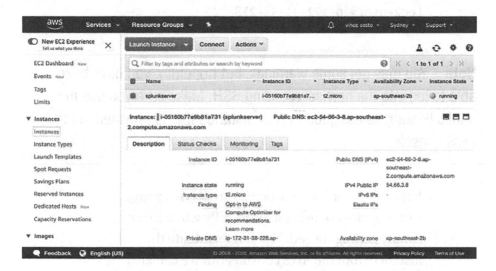

Figure 5-6. *Your New Splunk Server Instance Viewed from the AWS
Web Console*

16.   We made a copy of the keypair we created earlier in
this chapter, and this will allow us to now connect
to the newly created server. By using **SSH** and the
public IP address AWS has assigned to our new
server, we can now connect to our server with the
following command:

ssh -i splunkserver.pem ec2-user@<public_ip_address>

```
Last login: Tue Jul 21 23:36:42 2020 from 103.224.107.5
       _|  _|_  )
       _|  (     /    Amazon Linux AMI
       _|\___|___|
```

```
https://aws.amazon.com/amazon-linux-ami/2018.03-
release-notes/
29 package(s) needed for security, out of 64 available
Run "sudo yum update" to apply all updates.
[ec2-user@ip-172-31-38-228 ~]$
```

Note   You may get some warnings, but hopefully, you have been able to log into the new server using SSH. Make sure you use the public IP address assigned to your instance that is provided in the AWS console.

---

17.   Finally, we don't want to keep our service going when we are not using it, especially while we are simply getting started. You can terminate the instance from the AWS console, but we can also use Ansible in the command line. All we need is the AWS instance ID, which is a 17-character value assigned to your new server. Run the following command that uses the **ec2** Ansible module and uses the arguments of **instance_ids** and AWS **region**, and the state changed to absent:

ansible localhost -m ec2 -a "instance_ ids=i-05160b77e9b81a731 region=ap-southeast-2 state=absent"

```
localhost | SUCCESS => {
    "changed": true,
    "instance_ids": [
        " i-05160b77e9b81a731"
    ],
```

```
...
    ],
    "tagged_instances": []
}
```

We have once again reduced the amount of output on our page, but you should be able to head to your AWS console and see your server is now either terminated or in the process of shutting down. Once again, the preceding example uses the instance ID provided to us, and you will need to use the ID provided to you via the console, and once terminated, the server will not be able to be accessed again.

If you're wondering why we are already terminating our server even though we have not installed Splunk on it yet, well this is the benefit of using immutable hardware. In the following section, you will see we will be able to fully provision the server, with Splunk installed, all using Ansible and without having to make any changes to the server itself.

Deploying Splunk with User Data

We almost have our running server up and working, but without the Splunk application running on the server, it is not really complete. Since we have been automating all our installations, we will do the same with our Splunk installation. In this case, though, we can use Amazon's user data to complete the installation once our instance has been created.

If you don't have any experience with user data before, don't worry; we are going to make it pretty simple, and of course, we will be using our Ansible role to automate the process. Basically speaking, user data is a simple automation script which is run the first time the instance is created.

We don't have to add too much more to our splunk_server role to get it working, so access your working environment and we can get started:

1. Start by creating our **user_data.sh** file which we will then call by our splunk_server role tasks. This will be located in the **roles/splunk_server/files** directory, so run the following command to create the new file:

touch roles/splunk_server/files/user_data.sh

2. There are only six lines to our user data script, but there are some long URLs in it, so open the user_ data.sh with your text editor and add the following details to the script:

```
1 #!/bin/bash
2 set -e -x
3 wget -O splunk-8.2.6-a6fe1ee8894b-linux-2.6-x86_64.
  rpm "https://download.splunk.com/products/splunk/
  releases/8.2.6/linux/splunk-8.2.6-a6fe1ee8894b-
  linux-2.6-x86_64.rpm"
4 rpm -i splunk-8.2.6-a6fe1ee8894b-linux-2.6-x86_64.rpm
5 sleep 30
6 sudo -u splunk /opt/splunk/bin/splunk
       start  --answer-yes --no-prompt --accept-
       license  --seed-passwd newpassword
```

Lines 1 and 2 allow your script to be executable by our new instance, and line 3 uses the **wget** command to grab the Splunk installation file from the Splunk website. Lines 4 and 5 then install the application using the **rpm** package manager and wait for 30 seconds to make sure the installation is

complete. Lastly, the Splunk application is started by
accepting all installation questions as **yes**, accepting
the license agreement, and seeing the admin user
password as "newpassword."

Note   As of writing this, the latest version of Splunk was version
8.2.6. If this version is no longer available by the URL attached, you
may need to obtain the URL from the Splunk website:
www.splunk.com.

Please note you will need to register with the site to obtain the latest
version and URL to download it from. Please also note the preceding
installation is using the RPM package manager as we are using an
Amazon Linux image. If you are using a different image type, you may
need to use a different package manager such as APT.

---

3. To allow our splunk_server role to use the user_data.
    sh script during installation, all we need to do is
    reference it from our tasks file we created earlier.
    Using your favorite text editor, open the **roles/
    splunk_server/tasks/main.yml** file.

4. You will need to move down to the middle of the file
    where we have named our task **"launch the new ec2
    instance"**; at the end of this section, you will need to
    add in line 34 which we have highlighted:

```
33    count: 1
34    user_data: "{{ lookup('file', 'user_data.sh') }}"
35  register: ec2
```

Line 34 adds the **user_data.sh** file to run once the instance starts up and references the new file that we created in our files directory of our splunk_server role. If you are using the GitHub repository, we have created a separate main.yml file with the changes and named it main-v2.yml in the code for Chapter 5.

5. Just as we did earlier, we can run our playbook from the command line with the following command, this time being run with the **-v** option to let us see some extra output:

ansible-playbook -i hosts server_deploy.yml -v

```
PLAY [localhost]
...
om", "public_ip": "13.236.119.194", "ramdisk": null,
"region": "ap-southeast-2", "ro\
ot_device_name": "/dev/xvda", "root_device_type":
"ebs", "state": "running", "state_\
code": 16, "tags": {}, "tenancy": "default",
"virtualization_type": "hvm"}, "msg": "\
Tags {'Name': 'splunkserver'} created for resource
i-07d5243abda19d984."}
PLAY RECAP ********************************
localhost:
ok=4    changed=2    unreachable=0    failed=0
```

We've cut out a lot of output, but you will notice the public IP address we have highlighted in the output. This can be used to now access the web interface of our newly created Splunk server.

Note   Our server may be displaying as up and running on our AWS console; the actual Splunk web interface may still be taking a little while to start up. So you may need to be a little patient and leave two to three minutes to allow Splunk to start, especially because we are using a smaller AWS EC2 instance type.

6. To access the new installation, open a web browser, and enter the following URL, substituting your public IP address for the following one:

    `http://<public_ip_address:8000>`

7. If your playbook has run successfully, you should be prompted with a Splunk login screen where you can enter "**admin**" as the username and the seed password of "**newpassword**" we set up as part of our user_data.sh and should look like the image in Figure 5-7.

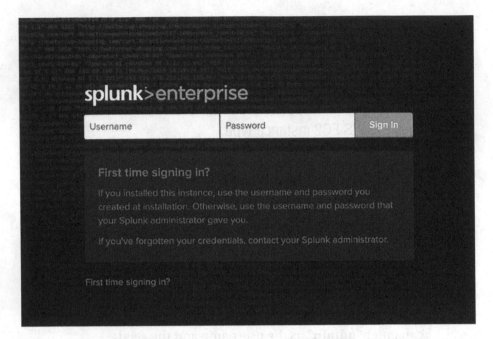

Figure 5-7. *The Login Screen for Your Splunk Web Interface*

8. If everything has worked out like it was supposed
    to, you should now be logged into your new Splunk
    installation and see a screen similar to the one in
    Figure 5-8.

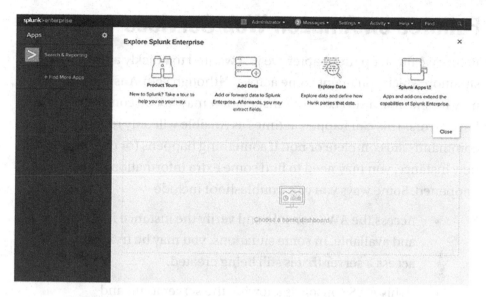

Figure 5-8. The Welcome Screen for Your Splunk Web Interface

9. Just before we finish up our work for the chapter, remove the running instance from AWS so we no longer incur costs from it running. Run the following command as we did earlier in the chapter using the instance ID for your running instance to make sure the server is stopped and terminated:

    ansible localhost -m ec2 -a "instance_ids=<your_ instance_id> region=ap-southeast-2 state=absent"

Our Splunk installation is looking pretty good, but we still have some work to do over the next chapters to get it working the way we want it to. For now, we have a brief discussion on how you can start to troubleshoot issues with your AWS and Ansible deployments before finishing off the chapter.

Failures on Amazon Web Services

Before we finish up the chapter, we just wanted to quickly address one situation which you might come across. Although your Ansible output may be showing a success, your installation may not be complete or might have errors. This can happen at times as Ansible will only report if its commands are complete or not. If something happens (or doesn't) on the new instance, you may need to find some extra information on what has happened. Some ways you can troubleshoot include

- Access the **AWS console** and verify the instance is up and available. In some situations, you may be trying to access a server that is still being created.

- If this AWS console is showing the server as up and running, you can also see further details on the console. You can select the instance from the console and click the **Actions** menu. From here, select **Instance Settings** and then click **Get System Log** which will hopefully show you the system log of your system without actually needing to log onto or SSH to the server.

- If you can log onto the new server, do so and view the **/var/log/cloud-init-output.log** or **/var/log/cloud-init.log** for errors. These logs will show the system logs for the server starting up including the progress of the user_data.sh file that may be running.

- Access the application logs you want to start up, in our case Splunk; you would check the logs in the **/opt/splunk/var/log/splunk/** directory. There are numerous logs in this directory, all of which could point to an issue with the application.

It may be the last thing you would want to happen, but by systematically approaching your installation, you can start to verify each step of the process is complete before moving onto the next. This is the basic way of troubleshooting your installation but hopefully something you will not need to rely on too much.

Summary

We've done a lot of work in this chapter and covered off a lot of new concepts, not just with Ansible, but other technologies like AWS, AWS CLI, and Splunk. We started our chapter with a discussion on Amazon Web Services and why we decided to use AWS compared to other cloud services. We then went through some of the basics of AWS and how to gain access to an account. We then discussed how we can start to use AWS with Ansible and also introduced the new project we are taking on in this and the following chapters.

With this in mind, we then started on our project, setting up our access and our AWS account, and started to work on creating our Amazon EC2 instance. We then used AWS user data files to perform and automate our new Splunk installation. Finally, we then had a quick discussion on what you need to look for when things can go wrong with our AWS deployments.

Our next chapter will continue our work with AWS expanding our server role further and allowing us to create an instance image we can then distribute across different environments. We will also work with the ansible-pull command which will give you the power to also download code and deploy it from a repository. There's a lot more exciting stuff coming, so keep reading.

CHAPTER 6

Ansible Templates and CloudFormation Scripts

It's been pretty cool how far we've been able to automate our instance deployments all while using code. But we haven't finished yet; there is still more we can do with Ansible, especially when using Amazon Web Services. We could almost dedicate an entire book to using Ansible with AWS, so this is why we haven't stopped with just the previous chapter.

In this chapter, we are going to continue with our new project and take it further with built-in apps, preconfigured users, and configurations when the instance is deployed. In this chapter, we are going to cover these:

- We will start by introducing **templates** within our Ansible roles and get you started with some of the basic features of using them with your infrastructure management.

- Then, we will expand these concepts by introducing a little-known feature of Ansible called **ansible-pull**.

- We will then create our own server image using Ansible which we can then deploy and further reduce our time to deployment.

© Vincent Sesto 2022
V. Sesto, *Practical Ansible*, https://doi.org/10.1007/978-1-4842-8643-2_6

- Finally, we will create a new Ansible role where we will work with **CloudFormation** templates to incorporate our newly created image.

So I hope you are ready for more. I don't think the work we will be doing is more complicated than anything we have done previously, but will hopefully show you how far Ansible can be expanded.

One Final Word on AWS Costs

I know I've said this three times already and I promise this is the last time you will hear me mention it again. The last thing we would want is for someone to get an unexpected bill from Amazon after working through the examples in these chapters. You always need to make sure you are cleaning up your instances and the AWS services you have deployed once they are no longer in use. If you are unfamiliar with the AWS web console billing service, it provides an easy way to monitor how much you are using and your expected cost you'll be billed by the end of the month.

If you haven't logged into your AWS console, do so and you then go to the URL `https://console.aws.amazon.com/billing/home`.

You may need to have specific privileges with your Amazon account, but if you can access it successfully, you should see your account **Billing and Cost Management Dashboard**. From here, you will get a number of graphs and be able to see numerous statements and tables concerning your account. One of the main images you will see is similar to the one in Figure 6-1, which is my account balance for the month of July 2020.

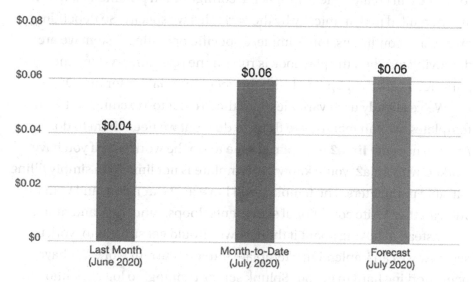

Figure 6-1. *The AWS Billing and Cost Management Dashboard*

So please be mindful of the costs you are incurring when using AWS. Now that we have covered costs one last time, we can move back to our Splunk server deployment project, with the following section allowing us to demonstrate the use of templates within our project.

Ansible Templates in AWS Instances

I'm not sure if you've been thinking about the way we've been working. In some instances, we could be reducing the amount of work we are doing by using code to create our configuration instead of constantly writing them. Especially when our environments change, if we move from a development environment to a production environment, we want to limit the configurations we are setting up. One way to do this is with the use of **Ansible templates**.

When we introduced roles as part of our previous chapter, we showed the template file as being part of the role directory structure, but we didn't really go into any further detail until now. By using templates as part of our roles, we can create a file with specific configuration parameters, which are then filled in dynamically by the variables we specify. So depending on specific conditions, for example, a specific operating system we are deploying to, when the playbook is run on the operating system, the parameters are then updated with the specific variables for that OS.

We've already used variables, and they're not too exciting, but with templates, we can manipulate them to do what we need them to do. Ansible uses the **Jinja2** template engine to do the work, and if you have worked with Jinja2, you'll know the template is not limited to simply filling variable parameters. The template will have a **.j2** extension, and with it, you can then write conditional statements, loops, functions, and more.

Instead of talking about it though, we should get straight to work to see how we can implement a template into our current work. We have been working hard to get our Splunk server running, so log back into your working environment and we will enhance our deployment with a template:

1. Before we start making changes to our code, make sure you have removed any instances you've created from the previous chapters as we are going to create a new AWS instance from our code.

2. We want to make a change to the way our **splunk_server** role works; instead of using the files directory for our **user_data** script, we want to start using a template. Start by using your text editor to open the **roles/splunk_server/tasks/main.yml** file.

3. Move down to line 34 and make the following
    change to the file. Line 34 is now a little different as
    it is now using the **lookup** function to find the **user_
    data.j2** template in the template directory instead of
    the file we originally created:

```
33      count: 1
34      user_data: "{{ lookup('template',
        'user_data.j2') }}"
35   register: ec2
```

4. Create a templates directory in our splunk_server
    role. Run the following mkdir command to create a
    templates directory ready for us to start creating our
    Jinja2 template:

mkdir roles/splunk_server/templates

5. We can now create our template file and will use
    our current **user_data.sh** file as the base of our
    template. We can add extra template functionality
    as we go, but to get it started, copy the original **user_
    data.sh** file into our **templates** directory, but this
    time, we will use the **.j2** file extension:

**cp roles/splunk_server/files/user_data.sh roles/
splunk_server/templates/user_data.j2**

6. In our last chapter, we created our **admin** account
    when we started our Splunk server, but we used
    a plain text password in our user_data.sh file. We
    can start to set up our template by changing this

line to a variable. Open your template file **roles/
splunk_server/templates/user_data.j2** with your
text editor and change line 6 to now use the variable
admin_password:

```
6 sudo -u splunk /opt/splunk/bin/splunk start
--answer-yes --no-prompt --accept-license --seed-passwd
{{ admin_password }}
```

7. We can also use loops within our template, so this
   will be a perfect way we can add some more users to
   our installation. We should have our **user_data.j2**
   file open in our text editor, so we can then add the
   following loop to our template:

```
 8 {% for item in userlist %}
 9    sudo -u splunk /opt/splunk/bin/splunk add user
      {{ item }} -role admin -auth admin:{{ admin_
      password }}
10 {% endfor %}
```

Splunk allows you to create new users via the
command line with the **add user** command, but we
also need to provide the admin user password. In
this instance, line 8 will loop through the values in
the userlist variable and will add a new user account
for each in line 9. Line 10 then closes off our loop.

8. Save the **user_data.j2** template file as we have
   completed the work we are going to do on that
   file for now. We can now enter the variables this
   template will use, so open the **roles/splunk_server/
   vars/main.yml** file with your text editor.

9. We should be creating a separate list for users and
    then a separate list for password; instead, we have
    cut some corners a little by adding the username
    and password in the same entry, so when the loop
    runs in our template, the **userlist** will complete
    the add user command that runs in the user_data
    template loop. Add in the following details which
    add the admin_password into the variables file, and
    line 8 adds three users which we have named as
    user1, user2, and user3:

```
7 admin_password: newpassword
8 userlist: ['user1 -password changeme1', 'user2 -password
  changeme2', 'user3 -password changeme3']
```

10. The variables in the splunk_server role now contain
    sensitive information, so we will encrypt the data
    before we perform a deployment of our code.
    Just like we learned earlier in this book, we will
    use the **ansible-vault** command to encrypt our
    variables file:

```
ansible-vault encrypt roles/splunk_server/vars/main.yml
```

```
New Vault password:
Confirm New Vault password:
Encryption successful
```

11. Hopefully, everything has been set up correctly
    and we can now deploy our changes into a new
    environment. Let's run our playbook; this time,
    make sure you are providing the Ansible Vault

password you created in the previous step. As you can see, we add the **--ask-vault-pass** as part of our command:

**ansible-playbook -i hosts server_deploy.yml
--ask-vault-pass**

```
Vault password:

PLAY [localhost] ***********************************
TASK [splunk_server : Create the host security
group]******
ok: [localhost]

TASK [splunk_server : launch the new ec2 instance]
********
changed: [localhost]
TASK [splunk_server : wait for SSH to come up] ********
ok: [localhost] => (item={u'kernel': None, u'root_
device_type': u'ebs',
...
u'instance_type': u't2.micro', u'architecture':
u'x86_64', u'hypervisor': u'xen'})
TASK [splunk_server : add tag to instance] ************
changed: [localhost] => (item={u'kernel': None, u'root_
device_type': u'ebs',
...
u'instance_type': u't2.micro', u'architecture':
u'x86_64', u'hypervisor': u'xen'})
PLAY RECAP ********************************************
localhost:
ok=4     changed=2     unreachable=0     failed=0
```

12. Once again, our Splunk server should now be
     provisioned and running, and after a couple of
     minutes, the web interface should also be available.
     We should have four users available to access our
     server, and we could simply test the usernames by
     logging in directly to the web interface. Instead, log
     into the web interface using the admin user, and we
     will view our list of users in the User Administration
     screen of Splunk. We should be able to log into
     the web interface by using the external IP address
     provided by the AWS console and port 8000. Use the
     admin username and password to log into the web
     interface:

```
http://<Public IP>:8000
username: admin
password: newpassword
```

13. At the top right of the Splunk web interface, click the
     Settings menu and click the **Users** option. When
     you click the Settings menu, you should see a drop-
     down menu similar to the one in Figure 6-2, where
     you can select the User and Roles option.

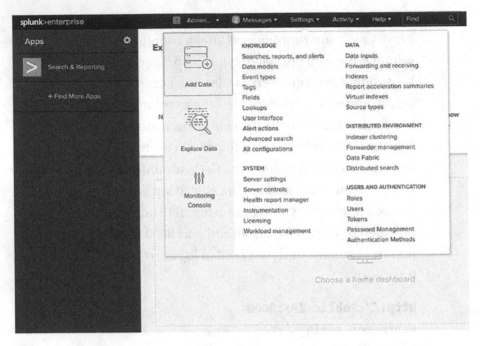

Figure 6-2. *The Splunk Web Interface Settings Menu*

14. Now when you view the users on your Splunk
    server, you should now be presented with a list of
    users similar to the one in Figure 6-3; we have four
    users automatically provisioned for us as part of our
    installation.

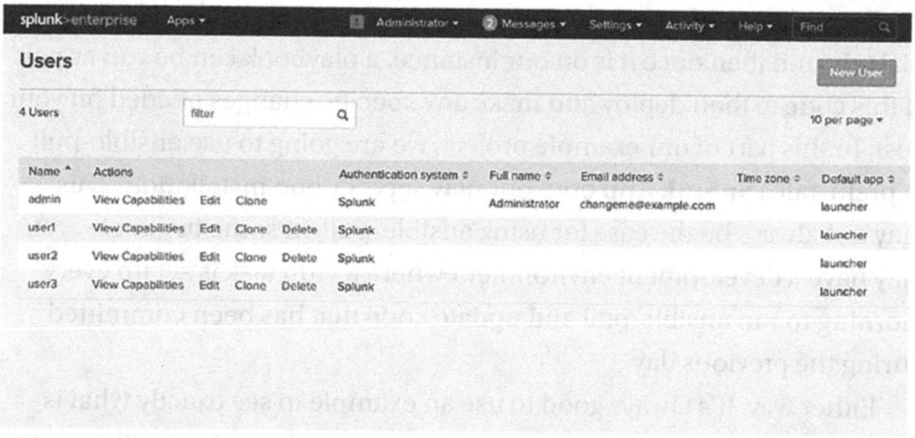

Figure 6-3. *A Listing of Preconfigured Users in Your Splunk Instance*

As you can see, templates allow us some extra flexibility to configure numerous users without needing to manually enter their details. This could be extended further to other configurations needed as well as setting up different variables for different environments. For now, though, we will change our focus to see other methods of provisioning our servers, in this instance, using Ansible Pull.

Pulling Code with Ansible

The first time I heard of this concept, it blew my mind, and the interesting thing is it is not documented very widely. It's probably because it is pretty basic, but can still do a lot of work for you and will address some interesting problems you have. So far, we've been using Ansible to create our AWS instance, but what if we then wanted to run Ansible on this new instance? Well of course, we can do this; we have our **user_data.j2** template which could simply install Ansible and then run specific commands, but in the following example, we are going to do something a little different to show you another feature of Ansible.

By using **ansible-pull**, we can use this command to pull code from **GitHub**, and then once it is on our instance, a playbook can be run as part of this code to then deploy and make any specific changes needed on your host. In this part of our example project, we are going to use ansible-pull to preinstall a **Splunk App** onto our new server upon installation. This may not always be the case for using ansible-pull; in some instances, you may have a development environment where a cron task is set up every morning to run ansible-pull and update code that has been committed during the previous day.

Either way, it's always good to use an example to see exactly what is going on, so log back into your working environment, and we will enhance our Splunk server role further to use the ansible-pull command:

1. Before we start making changes to our code, make sure you have removed any instances you've created from the previous chapters as we are going to create a new AWS instance from our code. As a reminder, we use the ec2 module with the AWS EC2 instance id with the following command:

    ```
    ansible localhost -m ec2 -a "instance_ids=<aws_
    instance_id> region=<aws_region> state=absent"
    ```

2. We already have our **user_data.j2** template running, so we'll be adding a few more lines to utilize **ansible-pull** within this template. Start by opening the **roles/splunk_server/templates/user_data. j2** file with your text editor, and move to the end of the file.

3. We first need to update our package manager to install all, **Git**, **Pip3**, and **Ansible**. As we are using Amazon Linux for our image, we will simply use the

yum commands, so add the following lines to our template we opened in the previous step:

```
12 sudo yum update -y
13 sudo yum install git python3-pip -y
14 sudo pip3 install ansible
```

4. Next, we can add in our ansible-pull command to our template which will import our repository of code we wish to install on our system. The **-U** option allows our code to be updated if it is already installed; the **ansible-pull** command will then run a **local.yml** playbook which is in the root of the repository code:

```
16 sudo /usr/local/bin/ansible-pull -U
     https://github.com/vincesesto/testsplunkapp -i hosts
```

Note   The repository we have used is already created, and we will run through it shortly to show you how everything works and how you can implement something similar into your projects.

---

5. Enter the following lines of code to finish off the **user_data.j2** template which will first enable Splunk to boot every time the server is restarted and then restart Splunk to allow our changes to take effect:

```
17
18 sudo /opt/splunk/bin/splunk enable boot-start
19
20 sudo -u splunk /opt/splunk/bin/splunk restart
21
```

6. Save the changes you have made to the user_data.j2
    template. The template file should now look similar
    to the following image where we have four distinct
    sections to our code and the setup of our server. We
    install Splunk and set up the basic configurations,
    we create and populate our users, we then install
    Ansible to allow us to run ansible-pull, and then
    finally, we set up the configurations around ansible-
    pull to deploy our basic Splunk App:

```
1 #!/bin/bash
2 set -e -x
3 wget -O splunk-8.2.6-a6fe1ee8894b-
  linux-2.6-x86_64.rpm "https://download.
  splunk.com/products/splunk/releases/8.2.6/
  linux/splunk-8.2.6-a6fe1ee8894b-
  linux-2.6-x86_64.rpm"
4 rpm -i splunk-8.2.6-a6fe1ee8894b-
  linux-2.6-x86_64.rpm
5 sleep 30
6 sudo -u splunk /opt/splunk/bin/splunk
  start --answer-yes --no-prompt --accept-
  license --seed-passwd {{ admin_password }}
7
8 {% for item in userlist %}
9   sudo -u splunk /opt/splunk/bin/splunk add
    user {{ item }} -role admin -auth admin:{{
    admin_password }}
10 {% endfor %}
11
12 sudo yum update -y
13 sudo yum install git python3-pip -y
```

```
14 sudo pip3 install ansible
15
16 sudo /usr/local/bin/ansible-pull -U https://
   github.com/vincesesto/testsplunkapp -i hosts
17
18 sudo /opt/splunk/bin/splunk enable
   boot-start
19
20 sudo -u splunk /opt/splunk/bin/
   splunk restart
```

If you are using the code from the GitHub repository, this file has been set up separately and named user_data_v2.j2.

7. We can now implement our changes. Run the following command line to run the playbook and create our Splunk server installation, this time with the prepopulated Splunk App installed from a GitHub repository:

```
ansible-playbook -i hosts server_deploy.yml --ask-
vault-pass
```

Note   Before you test your new instance, a lot of extra processes have been added into our server creation, including a Splunk restart, which will need to be run before you will be able to access the web interface. You can always SSH to the instance to verify it is working if you need to. Don't worry about the excessive time it takes to start up the server; we will work on fixing this later in this chapter.

Using the t2 micro, EC2 instance you may need to give it close to ten minutes for the full update and app installation to completely take place, so please be patient.

---

8. With a little extra time, you should be able to log into your new instance, just as you did previously by entering the following URL into your web browser: **http://<your_external_ip_address>:8000**

9. When you log onto your new Splunk server, although it will look similar to the previous times you have logged in, in this instance, you should now see a second app called **Ansible Answers App**, which has been installed and is visible on the left-hand menu of the Splunk web interface. Your installation should look similar to Figure 6-4 with the Ansible Answers App button visible below the Search & Reporting default app.

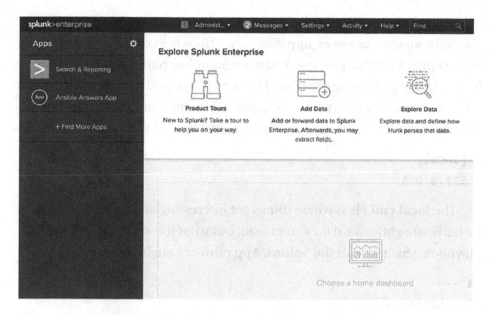

Figure 6-4. *The Splunk Web Interface with Preinstalled Apps*

This is a very simple example on how we can use ansible-pull to install an application and have it live on a running server when it starts up. The application being installed is running a simple Ansible playbook, which we will discuss and provide further details for in the following section.

Ansible Pull GitHub Repository Deployment Explained

We have saved a little time by creating the code to be deployed earlier with our **ansible-pull** request. If you download the repository from GitHub at **https://github.com/vincesesto/testsplunkapp**, you'll see there are only three files in the root of the repository:

- ansible_answers_app

- hosts

- local.yml

197

Unless you're really interested in Splunk Apps, you won't need to worry about the **ansible_answers_app** directory. This is the code which is the actual application that gets installed in on Splunk as part of our code. The **hosts** file though is being referenced by our ansible-pull command with the -i hosts, just as we would with a normal Ansible command. If we open the file, it is a simple hosts file referencing the local host, as you can see here:

```
1 [local]
2 127.0.0.1
```

The **local.yml** file is where things get interesting and by now should be fairly straightforward for you to work out what it is doing. It's a basic playbook which installs the **Splunk App** onto our environment:

```
1 ---
2 - hosts: all
3
4   tasks:
5   - name: install ansible splunk app
6     copy:
7         src: ansible_answers_app
8         dest: /opt/splunk/etc/apps/
9         owner: splunk
10        group: splunk
```

In the playbook, line 2 refers to all the servers in the hosts file and then runs one task to simply copy our **ansible_answers_app** directory, using the **copy** module into the Splunk applications folder, which is listed as our **dest**. It also changes the destination directory to be owned by the Splunk user and group, ready for the server to be restarted.

Although ansible-pull is limited with the options available to it, the playbook it can then download and run allows you to basically do anything you can with a regular Ansible playbook. The ansible-pull command does allow you to check out a different branch instead of the master branch and also set up different host files.

For more detail on the different options you can use with the ansible--pull command, please see the official documentation at the link https://docs.ansible.com/ansible/2.4/ansible-pull.html.

Build AWS Images for Quicker Deployments

For the past two chapters, we've been deploying our infrastructure on to AWS with no real complication, but one thing you may have noticed especially in the previous example is that the time it takes for our instance to be up and running has also increased with the amount of functionality we have added to the host.

We can put things into perspective for a moment as our latest server only took approximately five minutes to be up and running, configured with both users and applications running. But what if the applications were more complex and as a result extended the time it took to deploy our server? The good thing is Amazon gives you the option to prebuild your image and place it in their repository of images.

You'll remember when we first started working with Amazon Web Services, we used an **Amazon Linux image** to create our Splunk server. Now that we have all of our configuration management and code deployment working, we should be able to create an image from those servers. Having our own image should help improve the speed of our deployment, improve the stability of our server as we know it is stable before creating our image, and improve the portability as we have one simple image containing our server and all of its code.

We could simply use the AWS console to easily create our new image, but since we've been using Ansible all this time, why not use it again to create our new image? The cool thing is we can also make some changes to our Splunk installation, where we can add functionality to the installation by the way of allowing the API to be accessible. Then we can use the API to make sure our installation is complete before we create an image from our installation.

You'll see this is pretty easy, considering the knowledge you have gained so far, so log back into your working environment and we will make some further changes to our code:

1. Once again, before we start working on our changes, we make sure we have cleaned up the current Splunk server we created as part of the previous exercise.

2. We first need to enable the Splunk **API**. This is enabled by default as part of the current release of Splunk, but we have to allow AWS to communicate over port **8089**. So, start by opening the **roles/ splunk_server/tasks/main.yml** file with your text editor ready to add some extra functionality.

3. Move to line 15 where you have specified the port values to be open for port 8000. Add in the following four lines in bold to allow the API port of **8089** to also be allowed and accessible:

```
12          - proto: tcp
13            from_port: 8000
14            to_port: 8000
15            cidr_ip: 0.0.0.0/0
16          - proto: tcp
17            from_port: 8089
18            to_port: 8089
19            cidr_ip: 0.0.0.0/0
```

4. If we then move to the end of the file, we can now
    add in a task to wait for the changes to take effect in
    our **user_data.j2** file. In this instance, we will use
    the **uri** Ansible module to make an API call for our
    new Splunk App and to verify it has been installed:

```
58 - name: wait for service to be up and complete
59   uri:
60     url: "https://{{ ec2.instances[0].public_
       ip}}:8089/services/apps/local/ansible_
       answers_app"
61     validate_certs: no
62     user: admin
63     password: '{{ admin_password }}'
64     status_code: 200
65   register: result
66   until: result['status'] == 200
67   retries: 12
68   delay: 60
69
```

We have set up the URL in line 60 to use the instance
IP address assigned to our new host, assigning it
our **username** and **password** to allow access. We
are using the **uri** module in this instance, which will
continue to run until a status code of **200** is received.
Line 65 will register the results, and line 66 will allow
the URL to continue to be tested until we see a 200
value returned. Line 67 allows this to be attempted
12 times, with a 60-second delay specified in line 68.

5. When our role sees the API is working as we want it
    to, we can now use the **ec2_ami** module to create
    a new Splunk image from our installation. We
    simply need to provide the instance ID we are using
    as basis of our new image and provide name and
    description details:

```
70 - name: create ami for new Splunk servers
71   ec2_ami:
72     region: "{{ ec2_region }}"
73     instance_id: "{{ item.id }}"
74     name: "splunk-production"
75     description: "Production Splunk Deployment"
76     wait: yes
77   register: splunk_ami
78   with_items: '{{ ec2.instances }}'
```

As you can see, we have used the **with_items** option
to allow Ansible to loop through any number of
images we may have created during our script.

6. We are going to finish off our playbook tasks by
    deleting the live EC2 server instance we created,
    but you may want to leave this out. This will mean
    we will no longer be charged for the cost of a server
    we are not going to use any further. We simply use
    the ec2 module again, but this time, we set the **state**
    as **absent**:

```
80 - name: delete ec2 instance configured to create the
       Splunk server AMI
81   ec2:
82     region: "{{ ec2_region }}"
83     instance_ids: "{{ ec2.instance_ids }}"
84     state: absent
```

As a whole, the playbook now creates our Splunk server fully installed and configured with users and Splunk Apps and is allowing access to the build-in Splunk API. It will also create an AMI of the server and then remove the server we built to clean up everything ready to distribute our image across the world, ready for world like a server production line.

7. It's time to now run the playbook with all the new changes we've made, so let's kick it off and watch from afar and wait for the magic to happen:

ansible-playbook -i hosts server_deploy.yml --ask-vault-pass

8. When the playbook runs, as we mentioned in step 4 of this exercise, we made sure the playbook would wait for the server to be running and ready before it created the image. As we changed our code to perform 12 attempts with a 60-second delay in between each try, you'll notice the output of the playbook command we have just run should be showing something similar to the following output while it continues to test and verify the image is completed or not:

```
...
TASK [splunk_server : wait for service to be up
and complete] **********
FAILED - RETRYING: wait for service to be up
and complete (12 retries left).
FAILED - RETRYING: wait for service to be up
and complete (11 retries left).
FAILED - RETRYING: wait for service to be up
and complete (10 retries left).
FAILED - RETRYING: wait for service to be up
and complete (9 retries left).
FAILED - RETRYING: wait for service to be up
and complete (8 retries left).
FAILED - RETRYING: wait for service to be up
and complete (7 retries left).
...
```

9. Everything hopefully should have worked, and
    we should now have our environment cleaned up
    and no longer showing a live Splunk server, but
    we should see a new AMI available to launch from
    AWS. Log back into the AWS console and navigate to
    the EC2 console.

10. In the left-hand menu, if you select **AMIs** and as
    long as you are in the correct region, you should
    now see our new image available and ready for use.
    Figure 6-5 shows our AWS console with the new AMI
    available and named **splunk-production**.

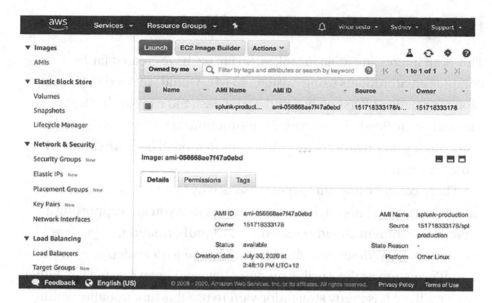

Figure 6-5. *Viewing Your Splunk Server Image Created in Your AWS Console*

Note   The AWS console displays an AMI ID for the image you have created. You will need to make note of the ID assigned to your image as this will be used to deploy new server using CloudFormation later in this chapter.

If you're not too familiar with AWS, you're probably wondering why the work we've done is important. The next section will run you through the process of using this newly created image. For now, just realize we are laying the foundations for a fast and stable server deployment.

Using CloudFormation with Ansible

This is an interesting topic to look at. So far, we have created fairly complex environments using Ansible, so why would we need to be using CloudFormation? Personally, I find it a lot easier to use Ansible from the start to the finish, but there will be situations where you will need to implement your environment with a combination of both **Ansible** and **CloudFormation**.

There could be any number of reasons why you may need to use CloudFormation. This might include the fact that you are supporting a legacy environment already created with CloudFormation, or you are creating a new AWS service which is only available to be deployed with CloudFormation as the Ansible modules have not been created yet. Either way, you'll see it is pretty straightforward to use this functionality within Ansible.

If you haven't used CloudFormation before, it is Amazon's way of managing infrastructure and configurations in AWS by providing **JSON** or **YAML** template files to describe the infrastructure. If you haven't seen a CloudFormation template before, you'll notice it's a lot more complex than Ansible code, but due to the fact it is supported by AWS, it is widely used.

It's a perfect time for us to introduce CloudFormation as we can now use the new AMI we have just created and deploy it across a new CloudFormation stack. We won't be going very far in depth with CloudFormation and presume you will download the template being used. Even though it is very basic, this book is not a tutorial on CloudFormation and the CloudFormation script itself is still rather large.

To view the CloudFormation template we are going to use, go to the following link:

```
https://raw.githubusercontent.com/vincesesto/ansibleanswers/
master/chapter6/roles/splunk_cloud/files/splunk-stack.yml
```

We could simply use the CloudFormation template directly with the AWS console to deploy our new AMI, but that would go against everything we've done already. Instead, we are going to create a new Ansible role that will deploy the AMI into AWS using the aforementioned CloudFormation script. Log back into your working environment, and we will now create a new Ansible role to deploy our Splunk AMI into a CloudFormation stack:

1. We created our roles directory in the last chapter, and as we need to create a new role, start by changing into this directory with the following command:

cd roles

2. Create the new role in our environment using the ansiblegalaxy command. Run the following command with the **init** option, and call the new role **splunk_cloud**:

ansible-galaxy init splunk_cloud
```
- splunk_cloud was created successfully
```

3. We know the ansible-galaxy command will do the work for us in setting up our directories and structure for the new role. To verify this, run the **tree** command to show the newly created directory structure of the new **splunk_cloud** role:

tree splunk-cloud/

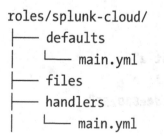
```
roles/splunk-cloud/
├── defaults
│   └── main.yml
├── files
├── handlers
│   └── main.yml
```

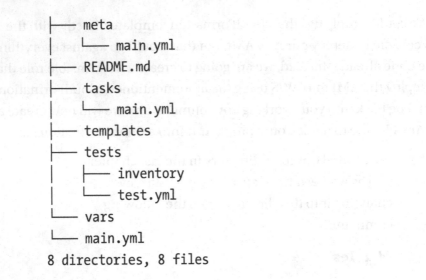

```
├── meta
│   └── main.yml
├── README.md
├── tasks
│   └── main.yml
├── templates
├── tests
│   ├── inventory
│   └── test.yml
└── vars
    └── main.yml
8 directories, 8 files
```

4. We will start by setting up some variables for our
    new environment, find your favorite text editor, and
    open the main variables file for the role located at
    splunk-cloud/vars/main.yml.

5. Enter the following variables which should be clear
    to you if you've been following along. The region
    and instance type are the same as our previous
    Splunk server deployment. Line 4 specifies the
    AMI we just created in the previous section; in our
    example, it was **ami-0a64e823d4e820755**, but you
    will need to change this to include the unique AMI
    identification number for your installation. Line 5
    is simply using the keypair we have been using to
    access our server:

```
1 ---
2 aws_region: "ap-southeast-2"
3 aws_instance_type: "t2.micro"
4 aws_image: "ami-0a64e823d4e820755"
```

```
5 aws_keypair: "ansible-answers-key"
6 aws_ssh_location: "0.0.0.0/0"
```

6. Save the details you've added to the variables file, and we can now set up our tasks to use the new variables. Open the **splunk_cloud/tasks/main.yml** file with your text editor.

7. Our tasks file should be a lot smaller than our previous tasks file, as we are using an image that will have all of the configurations created before it is deployed. So start with the following code. Line 3 uses the **cloudformation** module to construct the deployment through the AWS CloudFormation service. We start by naming the stack in line 4 as **ProdSplunkStack** and specifying the region from our variables in line 6:

```
1 ---
2 - name: start splunk cloudformation stack
3   cloudformation:
4     stack_name: "ProdSplunkStack"
5     state: "present"
6     region: "{{ aws_region }}"
```

8. The rest of the tasks file then uses the **template** option of the cloudformation module to define our stack template, using the parameters we have created in our variables file. Line 7 specifies the location of the template, and then lines 8–12 provide the parameters we would have needed to address when using the AWS CloudFormation console.

Finally, lines 13–16 provide tags to the stack and register the environment:

```
7       template: "roles/splunk_cloud/files/splunk-
        stack.yml"
8       template_parameters:
9         KeyName: "{{ aws_keypair }}"
10        InstanceType: "{{ aws_instance_type }}"
11        SSHLocation: "{{ aws_ssh_location }}"
12        AWSAMI: "{{ aws_image }}"
13        tags:
14          env: "Production"
15          service: "Splunk"
16      register: production_splunk_stack
```

9. If you haven't downloaded the CloudFormation template from GitHub, you can copy the template into the files directory of our role by running the following **wget** command, using the -O option to specify where the file will be placed; in the following command, we have specified the files directory of the splunk_cloud role:

```
wget https://raw.githubusercontent.com/vincesesto/
ansibleanswers/master/chapter6/roles/splunk_cloud/
files/splunk-stack.yml -O splunk_cloud/files/
splunk-stack.yml
```

Note   You will need to have the **wget** command available on your
working environment. The preceding command will download the raw
file from GitHub and place it in the splunk_cloud/files/ directory.

---

10. The role to deploy our Splunk server image to
     CloudFormation is now complete. Move back into
     the main working directory so we can finish off the
     final stages of this exercise:

     cd ../

11. Create a new playbook called **cloudformation_
     deploy.yml** which will use the role we have just
     created. Run the following command to create the
     playbook:

     touch cloudformation_deploy.yml

12. Open the file with your text editor and add the
     following code, which will run the new **splunk_
     cloud** role:

```
1 ---
2 - hosts: localhost
3   connection: local
4   gather_facts: false
5   user: root
6   roles:
7     - splunk_cloud
```

13.   We can now run our new playbook and see our
       CloudFormation stack created, so run the following
       ansible-playbook command to run the playbook we
       created in the previous step:

```
ansible-playbook -i hosts cloudformation_deploy.yml
```

14.   The stack should be up and running in one or two
       minutes. We can verify it is running by going to the
       AWS console, specifically for CloudFormation at the
       following URL:

```
https://ap-southeast-2.console.aws.amazon.com/
cloudformation
```

15.   Hopefully, you should see a new stack called
       ProdSplunkStack. If you select the stack on the
       console and click the **Events** tab, you should see a
       similar image to Figure 6-6, where you will notice
       from start to **CREATE COMPLETE**, CloudFormation
       has created our server in less than a minute to
       complete.

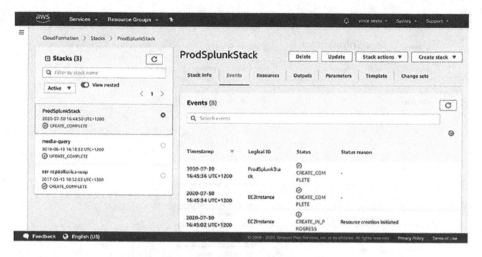

Figure 6-6. *Stack Create Events in AWS CloudFormation*

16.   If you then click the **Outputs** tab on the
CloudFormation console, you will also have the
PublicIP where you can now access your new
Splunk server. Once again, everything should be set
up and working with configured user access and
our sample Splunk App. Figure 6-7 is an example
of what the Outputs tab will look like for us in the
CloudFormation console.

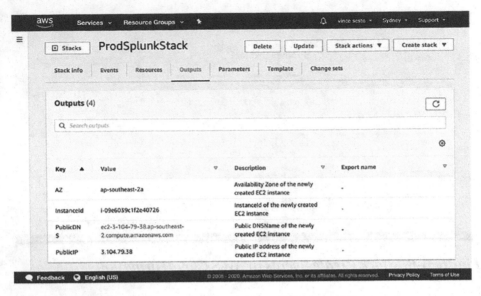

Figure 6-7. *Viewing Stack Outputs in AWS CloudFormation*

17.   In our example, we simply need to type the **PublicIP**
address along with the Splunk web port of **8000**
(http://3.104.79.38:8000) into our web browser to
access the new stack we have just implemented.
Figure 6-8 shows the Splunk web interface again as
it should now look similar with the preconfigured
AMI image deployed via CloudFormation.

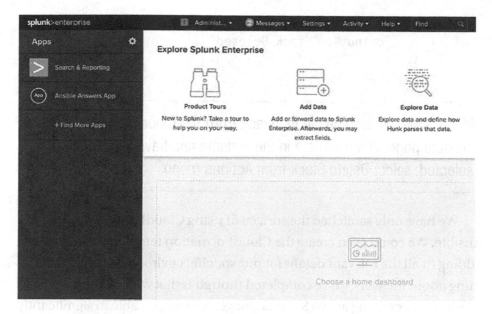

Figure 6-8. *Viewing Stack Outputs in AWS CloudFormation*

18.   Finally, we should delete this stack so you are no
longer incurring any costs from AWS. Run the
following command which uses the cloudformation
Ansible module and parses the stack_name and
region to the module and sets the state of the
CloudFormation stack as absent:

```
ansible localhost -m cloudformation -a
"stack_name=ProdSplunkStack region=
ap-southeast-2 state=absent"
localhost | CHANGED => {
    "changed": true,
    "events": [],
    "log": [
        "Stack does not exist."
```

```
        ],
        "output": "Stack Deleted"
    }
```

Note   You can also delete the stack from the CloudFormation AWS console page. When you are in the console and have your Stack selected, select Delete Stack from Actions menu.

We have only scratched the surface of using CloudFormation with Ansible. We could even create the CloudFormation templates with Jinja2, adding in all the relevant details for our specific environment. The great thing about the work we've completed though is that with a little bit of thought and creating an AWS server image, we've been able to significantly reduce the code we are using in Ansible and reduced the amount of time needed to deploy our code.

As this brings us to the end of this chapter, I think this should still get you moving in the right direction to make an implementation like this in your own project.

Summary

Our project is starting to look pretty epic, and we are setting up and automating a lot of processing in a small amount of code. I hope this is giving you an interesting and in-depth view on the power of Ansible and working with AWS. In this chapter, we have expanded on our previous AWS Splunk Instance and started to use Jinja2 templates as part of our work. In this section, we have also used the ansible-pull command to then bring in further GitHub repository code to allow our server to build with the latest version of our Splunk App.

We then moved on to simplifying things further by creating an AWS image from our server installation, which was then added to our CloudFormation template to create our production environment to help reduce the time to deployment. Our next chapter will allow us to start testing our Ansible code to make sure it is as correct as possible before performing any implementations.

## CHAPTER 7

Ansible Troubleshooting and Variables

We're almost at the end of our Splunk server project, and we hope you keep working through this chapter because there are a lot of extra details we are going to provide you to hopefully make your life and work a little easier.

In this chapter, we'll provide you with some tools and tips to make your Ansible code and configuration management a little easier. We are going to run through some of the ways you can provide extra details in your deployment code and roles and how to use these extra details to debug your playbooks. We are going to fill in some of the missing information you may have been asking yourself along the way.

There are a lot of details to fill in here, but we are hopefully going to make it a lot easier for you to manage your Ansible work. In this chapter

- We are going to start with a discussion on why AWS-specific playbooks need to use their own specific modules and not our usual Ansible modules and then give you some ideas on how to work around this.

- We will then learn some of the ways we can use variables and **facts** within your playbooks to help **debug** and provide information to the user as they run.

- We will also take a look at the **ansible-lint** project and how you can develop your own tests to work with the application.

- Finally, we will spend some time working with some of the more unknown options we are able to use with our playbooks, including options to help debug and verify everything is good before we release our code into the wild.

So let's not wait much longer as we've come a long way and your Ansible knowledge should have drastically increased from when you started in this journey.

AWS Modules Run Differently

I'm not sure if you've noticed, but we do things a little differently when working in the Amazon Cloud. If you think back to the early chapters of this book, we created our hosts file with an IP address, so our playbooks would then be able to map directly to the systems it needed to then configure. The reason we can't do this in the Amazon Cloud is that every time we launch a new instance, we create a new IP address for the instance. To reduce costs, we make sure we also shut down or terminate these hosts when they are no longer needed.

Once we have a server running though, if we plan to keep it up for as long as possible, we can also use Ansible as we have previously to manage configurations and installations. All we need to do is add it to our hosts file.

If we have created a new server with the IP address of 13.210.127.1, we could set up our host file like the following entry:

```
3
4 [splunk_server]
5 13.210.127.1
```

This all looks correct, but we can test this as we did back in our first chapter with the **ping** Ansible module:

```
ansible -i hosts "splunk_server," -m ping
```

```
13.210.127.148 | UNREACHABLE! => {
    "changed": false,
    "msg": "Failed to connect to the host via ssh:
    ansible@13.210.127.1: Permission \
    denied (publickey).\r\n",
    "unreachable": true
}
```

As you can see, we get an error showing the server as being UNREACHABLE. So what went wrong here?

We need to remember we first access the host via SSH with the **ec2-user** username because it is an AWS host, and secondly, we have set up an access key to access this which may not be in the default ssh key directory.

What I didn't show you in our earlier chapters is we can set up our hosts file with the location of the ssh key and the user who needs to access the host to make changes. If you open up the hosts file again and add the **ansible_ssh_private_key_file** location and the **ansible_ssh_user** value, this should help, as you will see in the following:

```
3
4 [splunk_server]
5 13.210.127.1 ansible_ssh_private_key_file=ansible-answerskey
  ansible_ssh_user=ec2-user
```

If we now run our test command, we should see a better result this time:

```
ansible -i hosts "splunk_server," -m ping
13.210.127.1 | SUCCESS => {
    "changed": false,
    "ping": "pong"
}
```

This isn't the best way to use Ansible, especially in AWS, but if you need to get something running quickly and have your playbooks set up with no specific entries relating to AWS, it may be a way to get you working a little faster. As well, if you are working on different systems and need to run your Ansible commands, it may be wise to make these entries in your hosts file.

Note   Amazon does have the option to use a permanent IP address and refer to it as an **Elastic IP**. It is beyond the scope of this book and doesn't really conform with the feel of the book, so we haven't covered it. If you are interested though, you can use the **ec2_epi** module to first create an Elastic IP, and you would then need to create an instance and assign this IP address to the instance. You could then continue to use the host file with the traditional Ansible playbook modules.

Using the Debug Module with Registered Variables

We have used the **debug** module in the previous chapters of this book, but will take some extra time to discuss it further in this section of the chapter. The debug module is basically a way Ansible allows you to print statements to your screen. In some situations, we would use a verbose output to allow us to see extra detail, as well as verify if our playbooks have been completed. Instead, the debug module can allow you to provide customized statements printed to the screen when our tasks are performed.

Debug can also work with **registered variables**, like the ones we have already used in our previous examples, to provide further testing and verification if our tasks have worked correctly.

For example, in the following task, we added to **roles/splunk_server/ tasks/main.yml** and registered the output of our **uri** module to the variable named **result**. We then queried the value to know when the result value was 200 which allows us to know that our API was available:

```
62 - name: wait for service to be up and complete
63   uri:
64     url: "https://{{ ec2.instances[0].public_ip}}:8089/
       services/apps/local/ansible_answers_app"
65     validate_certs: no
66     user: admin
67     password: '{{ admin_password }}'
68     status_code: 200
69   register: result
70   until: result['status'] == 200
71   retries: 12
72   delay: 60
```

We could then use this variable with a debug message like the following one to verify our deployment has worked as we wanted it to:

```
- debug:
  msg: "API is now available and providing a {{
  result['status'] }} response"
```

So we use **register** to capture the output of a task to a variable, and then these values can be used when logging output to the screen or creating conditional statements within our playbooks. Some of the modules also have specific return values you can use to then test against, but we will look at this more later in the chapter.

To explain this further, we are going to start adding some more debug information onto our playbooks to allow it to display some more useful information to us. Log back into your working environment, and we will make some minor changes to our **splunk_cloud** playbook we created in our last chapter:

1. Start by opening the **roles/splunk_cloud/tasks/ main.yml** file with your text editor ready to make a change to our file.

2. Move to the end of the file and add lines 18 and 19 into our playbook. In the following code, line 18 uses the **debug** module which is essentially a new task, wherein the entry below will use the **var** option to output the variable we registered in line 16:

```
16    register: production_splunk_stack
17
18 - debug:
19       var: production_splunk_stack
```

3. If we now run this playbook, we will get a large amount of output as the data registered in the variable **production_splunk_stack** will include all the AWS information output by the module in our playbook. The output we have listed as follows has been reduced significantly due to the large amount of data provided by AWS:

```
ansible-playbook -i hosts cloudformation_deploy.yml
PLAY [localhost] ************************************
TASK [splunk_cloud : start splunk cloudformation
stack] ***
changed: [localhost]
TASK [splunk_cloud : debug] ****************************
ok: [localhost] => {
    "production_splunk_stack": {
...
    "resource_type": "AWS::EC2::SecurityGroup",
    "status": "CREATE_COMPLETE",
    "status_reason": null
            }
        ]
    }
}
```

4. We can do a little better with our playbook and limit the data that is being displayed in our output. First, delete the stack from our AWS console before we move further with the following command line:

```
ansible localhost -m cloudformation -a "stack_
name=ProdSplunkStack region=ap-southeast-2 state=absent"
localhost | CHANGED => {
    "changed": true,
    "events": [],
    "log": [
        "Stack does not exist."
    ],
    "output": "Stack Deleted"
}
```

225

5. Open the roles/splunk_cloud/tasks/main.yml file again and add the following changes. In the code, we have added line 20 which will only display the big block of data we displayed previously if we use the **-vv** option when we run our playbook. Lines 22 and 23 set up a new debug module, and this time use the **msg** option to print a message to the screen similar to the way you would use a print or echo statement in code. In this instance, you can see we are still using the registered variable of **production_splunk_stack**, but in this instance, it is using the value of the **PublicIP** listed in the **stack_outputs**:

```
17
18 - debug:
19     var: production_splunk_stack
20     verbosity: 2
21
22 - debug:
23     msg: "IP Address Value {{ production_splunk_
       stack.stack_outputs.PublicIP }}"
```

6. Save the changes you've made to the tasks, and now run your playbook again with the following command. This time we get a different output to our screen:

```
ansible-playbook -i hosts cloudformation_deploy.yml

PLAY [localhost] ***********************************
TASK [splunk_cloud : start splunk cloudformation
stack] ***
changed: [localhost]
TASK [splunk_cloud : debug] ************************
```

```
skipping: [localhost]
TASK [splunk_cloud : debug] *************************
ok: [localhost] => {
    "msg": "IP Address Value 52.65.207.29"
}
PLAY RECAP ******************************************
localhost  :
ok=2    changed=1    unreachable=0    failed=0
```

Firstly, you'll notice there is a lot less output, but it still provides some helpful information. We can see our first debug statement we added to our code is showing in our output as "**skipping**" as we have not used the **-vv** option in our command line, but then our second debug module runs and gives us the nice message of "**IP Address Value 52.65.207.29**".

So you can see here how we can set variable values after the task has run and then print the output we want to the screen. If you remember the output we had earlier when we registered all the values of our output, you may have noticed the variable output was in a dictionary form. When we register the value in our playbook, the variable will always be in the form of a **dictionary**, but we won't necessarily know what keys will be available in the dictionary.

Although the Ansible module documentation will give you some information on what keys to expect from the output of specific modules, this information is far from complete, and in most situations, it is easier to use debug as we did earlier to see what information is provided.

In our example earlier, we extracted the data we needed from the dictionary using the **dot notation**. You can also use **square brackets** as well ([ ]), so for our example, we could also use the following to output the PublicIP address:

```
production_splunk_stack['stack_outputs']['PublicIP']
```

If we really wanted to, we could even mix the dot and square bracket notation, but it's probably best to stick to one consistent method across your playbooks. Also, if you are trying to access a dictionary key that does not exist, your playbook will also fail.

Ansible Facts

When we've been running our playbooks, one of the first options we have in place is to **gather_facts**, and in all our playbooks so far, we have been setting this as false. We have done this to limit the kind of information we have in our output as well as to speed up our playbooks. When Ansible gathers facts, it is connecting to the instance it is running the playbook on and gathers information on the system including CPU architecture, operating system, IP addresses, memory info, disk info, and much more.

As we have been performing a lot of our work using AWS, we are running our playbooks on our local machine, and as a result, when we are gathering facts, we would simply be gathering facts on the system we are working from. This doesn't mean Ansible facts do not have a use.

There are a few things we can still do, so log back into your working environment, and we can demonstrate how you can use facts further in your own projects:

1. If we wanted to gather all the **facts** Ansible stores, we can use the **setup** module from the command line. If you still have your Splunk server running, you can use the IP address along with the access key to output the entire 450 lines of data Ansible will output. By running the following command, you should get a massive amount of data, which we have only provided a small subset to illustrate the process:

```
ansible all -i "ec2-user@52.65.207.29," -m
setup  --key-file "splunkserver.pem"
ec2-user@52.65.207.29 | SUCCESS => {
    "ansible_facts": {
        "ansible_all_ipv4_addresses": [
            "172.31.22.179"

        ...
    },
    "changed": false
}
```

2. The setup module also comes with a **filter** argument to allow you to extract data you specifically need; in this case, let's only provide processor information. Run the following command to use the same setup module request, but instead use **-a** to specify the filter argument and to only provide the **ansible_processor_vcpus** data to the screen:

```
ansible all -i "ec2-user@52.65.207.29," -m
setup  --key-file "splunkserver.pem" -a
"filter=ansible_processor_vcpus"
ec2-user@52.65.207.29 | SUCCESS => {
    "ansible_facts": {
        "ansible_processor_vcpus": 1
    },
    "changed": false
}
```

3. The previous examples have been used to show how we can gather facts for any hosts, but of course, we are working with ec2 instances. Ansible provides us with the **ec2_metadata_facts** module, so we can use

this to extract specific information relative to AWS ec2 instances. Run the following command which uses the ec2_metadata_facts module to extract the facts for the specific instance. Once again, our limited output provides us with information that is a lot more relevant to AWS instances:

```
ansible all -i "ec2-user@52.65.207.29," -m
ec2_metadata_facts --key-file "splunkserver.pem"
ec2-user@52.65.207.29 | SUCCESS => {
    "ansible_facts": {
        "ansible_ec2_ami_id": "ami-0492f4f561f7b5b7a",
        "ansible_ec2_ami_launch_index": "0",
        ...
    },
    "changed": false
}
```

4. We can also set our own facts within our playbooks. In the previous section, we displayed the new IP address of our new server; if we want to use these variables across other playbooks, we need to turn them into facts. Open the **roles/splunk_cloud/ tasks/main.yml** file with your text editor and we will set up our first fact.

5. Move to the bottom of the splunk_cloud tasks file, and add in the code we have listed as follows. We will use the **set_fact** module to, as you may have guessed, set a fact:

```
25 - name: set public IP address to be used by other
     playbooks
26   set_fact:
27     splunk_public_ip: "{{ production_splunk_stack.
       stack_outputs.PublicIP }}"
```

Note   The reason we would want to do this is that any variables we use or define will be valid on the host running the playbook until all the tasks are complete. This means any variables will not be passed to our playbooks. Just as we have created a debug msg in the previous section of this chapter, we have now set the same PublicIP address value to the fact **splunk_public_ip**. We can now use this in other playbooks.

6. We only use one other playbook in this exercise, and this is the **cloudformation_deploy.yml**. Open it with your text editor, and we will add the following data to the end of the file to hopefully use the new fact we have created in the previous step:

```
8 tasks:
9   - debug:
10       msg: "Production Server Public IP Address
         {{ splunk_public_ip }}"
```

7. If we now run this playbook again, we will see an extra task at the end of the output which will print the new fact we created to the screen:

```
ansible-playbook -i hosts cloudformation_deploy.yml
...
TASK [debug] ****************************************
```

```
ok: [localhost] => {
    "msg": "Production Server Public IP Address
    52.65.207.29"
}
```

Using variables and facts is a good start in providing extra information to users as configurations are being deployed. In the next section of this chapter, we will discuss the README.md file provided with Ansible roles, which gives you one of the best ways of providing extra information to a potential user.

Ansible Galaxy README Files

By now, you may have noticed each of the Ansible roles we created with the ansible-galaxy init command will create a default READM.md file that is located in the base of the Ansible role. In the example we've been working on, it is located in the roles/splunk_cloud/README.md file.

README files are not a new thing and you've probably used them for years, but they are a great way to provide users with all the information they need to start using the infrastructure code we have created.

Figure 7-1 shows the README.md file we have created for the splunk_cloud role for the project we are working on.

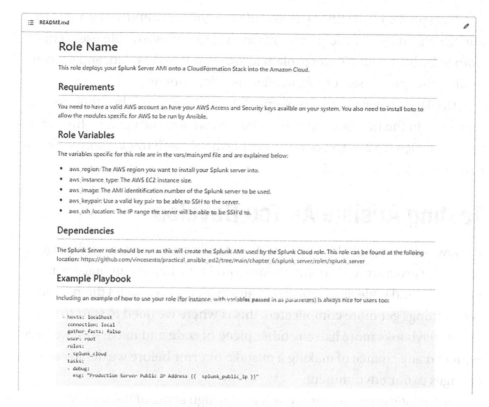

Figure 7-1. *The Splunk Cloud README.md File for Our Project*

We don't want to dwell on the README.md file for too long, but this will usually be the first thing a lot of users will look to when using your role. With only a short amount of time, you can put together a concise file that will give your users all the information they need to make sure they can support and use your roles.

From the image in Figure 7-1, we have used the prefilled values as a guide for setting up the README.md file for our splunk_cloud role, which include Requirements, Role Variables, Dependencies, Example Playbook, License, and Author Information.

The splunk_cloud README.md file is a good example as we need to add specific details for requirements as EC2 modules Ansible uses require Boto to be installed. We can explain all our variables needed, and we can outline the splunk_server role needed as a dependency.

All of this can make the implementation of your roles by other users a lot easier. In the next section of this chapter, we will start to look further at ways in which we can test our Ansible playbooks and roles before we need to actually deploy our code.

Testing Ansible As You Develop

By now, you can probably see Ansible not only creates a way to manage your infrastructure and configurations, but in itself, you can make your playbooks and code as complex and automated as you need them to be. When things get more complicated, this is where we need to start to look at our playbooks more like any other piece of code and make sure we have removed any chance of making a mistake or error before we deploy any changes to our environment.

In the following section, we will go through some of the tools you can use to test your code and make sure you are reducing any chance of issues before you run it in production. The cool thing is that, unlike other configuration management tools, Ansible works in order, so it will be easier for us to incorporate testing into our code and playbooks.

Ansible Start At Option

This isn't really a way to test our playbook, but it can come in handy. The **--start-at-task** option allows you to start the playbook at a particular task instead of running through all the other tasks first. It is useful if you have added a new task into a playbook and only want to run the specific task you have just created. All you need to do is list the task name, as illustrated in the following example.

234

We can use our existing project to demonstrate how to use this code, so log back into your working environment to get started:

1. Open the **cloudformation_deploy.yml** file with your text editor, and add the following three lines at the bottom of the playbook. All we are now doing in the playbook is adding a new task that will simply run the **debug** module to print some text to the screen:

```
11 - name: Final Task
12    debug:
13       msg: "This is the end of the playbook"
```

2. Now run the playbook with the following command which uses the --startattask option to specify that it is not going to run any of the other code in the playbook. As you can see, the output only runs one task, and this is the new debug message we have set up:

```
ansible-playbook -i hosts cloudformation_deploy.yml
   --start-at-task="Final Task"

PLAY [localhost] *******************************
TASK [Final Task] *******************************
ok: [localhost] => {
    "msg": "This is the end of the playbook"
}
PLAY RECAP *************************************
localhost:
ok=1    changed=0    unreachable=0    failed=0
```

Ansible Step

The **--step** option with **ansible-playbook** allows you to run your playbook interactively. Before each task is started, you will be asked if you would like to proceed with the task. You either answer yes or no or continue if you want the playbook to continue to the end without any further checks.

1. Run the following command to see how you can use the --step option with our current environment. As you can see, all that is needed is the --step option to be provided with our Ansible command. We are then prompted with options to proceed:

    ```
    ansible-playbook -i hosts cloudformation_deploy.
    yml --step
    ```

    ```
    PLAY [localhost]   ******************************
    Perform task: TASK: splunk_cloud : start splunk
    cloudformation stack (N)o/(y)es/(c)ontinue:
    ```

Ansible Lint

It is created by **Will Thames** (https://github.com/willthames) and is available on **GitHub** with only a small amount of documentation available. We will run through this rather quickly, but the defaults provide a lot of functionality to the application and will get you started.

The **ansible-lint** command takes your playbook and will check if your playbook conforms to the style guides and other rules to make sure you are minimizing the chances of your code-breaking something or not working correctly when you go to deploy your environment:

The GitHub repository for ansible-lint can be found at the following link: https://github.com/willthames/ansible-lint

In the following part of this exercise, we will install **ansible-lint** onto our system and then demonstrate the basic operations of the application:

1. Ansible-lint does not come installed as part of Ansible and will need to be installed into your system. Use the following command to install ansible-lint using the apt command for Linux/Debian-based environments:

    sudo apt install ansible-lint

Note   ansible-lint is written in Python, so if you are not running these commands on a system that includes apt, you can also use **pip3 install ansible-lint** to install the application on your system.

---

2. Run the following command to verify you have installed the ansible-lint application successfully. The following command is simply running ansible-lint with the --version option to verify the version installed:

    ansible-lint --version

    ansible-lint 4.3.7

3. Using ansible-lint is simple. All we need to do is run the command with a playbook that calls a role we would like to test. Run the following command to use **ansible-lint** with the **server_deploy.yml** playbook

we created in the previous chapter. The **-v** option
provides some extra details on the tasks occurring:

```
ansible-lint server_deploy.yml -v
```

```
[701] Role info should contain platforms
roles/splunk_server/meta/main.yml:1
{'meta/main.yml': {'galaxy_info': {'author': 'your
name', 'description':
```

```
[703] Should change default metadata: author
roles/splunk_server/meta/main.yml:1
{'meta/main.yml': {'galaxy_info': {'author': 'your
name', 'description':
```

```
[201] Trailing whitespace
roles/splunk_server/tasks/main.yml:69
...
```

You can skip specific rules or tags by adding them to
your configuration file:

```
# .ansible-lint
warn_list:  # or 'skip_list' to silence them completely
  - '201'  # Trailing whitespace
  - '206'  # Variables should have spaces
            before and after: {{ var_name
              }}
  - '701'  # meta/main.yml should contain relevant info
  - '703'  # meta/main.yml default values should be changed
```

The output provides guidance on anything incorrect in our playbook. As you can see from the preceding output, as our server_deploy.yml playbook is using the **splunk_server** role, it works through all of the files in this role. The output is not complete, but as you can see, it highlights a number of things in our code including role details, author details, and trailing whitespaces in the code.

4. If you know a little of Python, you can expand the rules being used by ansible-lint or create your own. In the following steps, we will set up a basic test using Python to make sure the lines of our code do not exceed 80 characters. Start by creating a directory for our rules called **test_rules**:

```
mkdir test_rules
```

5. Now create a new rule to look at the length of our Ansible code lines. Run the following command to create the file named LineLength.py to match the ansible-lint class we are going to create:

```
touch test_rules/LineLength.py
```

6. Open the test_rules/LineLength.py file with your text editor. Don't worry if you're not proficient with Python as we will provide details of what the code is doing and it will only run for 13 lines.

7. Add the following first two lines. In line 1, we import the **AnsibleLintRule** function from the **ansiblelint** module to then be used as part of our rule:

```
1 from ansiblelint import AnsibleLintRule
2
```

8. Add in lines 3–7 to set up our class name with an ansiblelint rule as ANSWERS01, descriptions, and tags for the new rule:

```
1 from ansiblelint import AnsibleLintRule
2
3 class LineLength(AnsibleLintRule):
4     id = 'ANSWERS01'
5     shortdesc = 'Line too long'
6     description = 'Python Code Style Guidelines
        Recommend Line Length Under 80 Characters'
7     tags = ['formatting']
8
```

9. Now add the final five lines to the new rule which creates a function to look through each line in our role and test if the line is longer than 80 characters, displaying to the screen if it does:

```
9     def match(self, file, line):
10        if len(line) > 80:
11            self.shortdesc += " ({} characters)".
              format(len(line))
12            return True
13        return False
```

10. Save the file so we can run the test we created. Our Ansible playbooks contain quite a few lines of code that are over 80 characters, so if we have set everything up correctly, we should see some errors

triggered. Run the following command over the
server_deploy.yml, this time using the -r option and
using the test_rules value, to ask ansible-lint to run
all the rules in this directory:

ansible-lint server_deploy.yml -r test_rules

[ANSWERS01] Line too long (95 characters)
roles/splunk_server/tasks/main.yml:60
    url: "https://{{ ec2.instances[0].public_ip}}:8089/
    services/apps/local/ansible_answers_app"

You can skip specific rules or tags by adding them to
your configuration file:

```
# .ansible-lint
warn_list:  # or 'skip_list' to silence them
completely
   - 'ANSWERS01'  # Line too long
   (95 characters)
```

11. If we had specific requirements that needed to be
    run for a role, we can also create a **configuration**
    file that can be run. ansible-lint allows us to specify

what should and shouldn't be run. Create the file
named **test_config.yml** as we have here, so we can
set up a sample configuration file:

```
touch test_config.yml
```

12.   Add the following details which will exclude the
specific paths in lines 2 and 3. It will use the test_
rules directory which is specified in lines 6 and 7,
and line 9 will use all the default rules as well when
running our tests:

```
1 ---
2 exclude_paths:
3   - roles/
4 parseable: true
5 quiet: true
6 rulesdir:
7   - test_rules/
8 use_default_rules: true
9 verbosity: 1
```

13.   Run ansible-lint again over the **server_deploy.
yml** file; this time, use the **-c** option to specify the
configuration file we created in the previous step.
We should get a lot fewer errors as we are now
excluding the roles directory from being viewed:

```
ansible-lint server_deploy.yml -c test_config.yml
```

```
Examining server_deploy.yml of type playbook
```

14. While we are using ansible-lint, we will take this opportunity to create another test; in this instance, we will see if we can test for AWS access keys that may be hard-coded in our Ansible roles. Create the new test by running the following command:

touch test_rules/AWSCredentials.py

15. Open the new file with your text editor and we can start creating our new rule. Add the following code with lines 1–8 that are very similar to the first rule we created where we import the AnsibleLintRule function and then set up the class with id and descriptions:

```
1 from ansiblelint import AnsibleLintRule
2
3 class AWSCredentials(AnsibleLintRule):
4     id = 'ANSWERS02'
5     shortdesc = 'Playbook May Contain AWS Cre-
      dentials'
6     description = 'AWS credentials should not be
      included in variables, especially if they are
      stored publically'
7     tags = ['formatting']
8
```

16. Add in the new function which runs in lines 9–17. The function simply runs two if statements that look for two specific words, **aws_access_key_id** and **aws_secret_access_key**. This is a very basic way to

do this check, but it should give you an example of
how to add in your own checks into ansible-lint:

```
9     def match(self, file, line):
10        if "aws_access_key_id" in line:
11            self.shortdesc
12            return True
13
14        if "aws_secret_access_key" in line:
15            self.shortdesc
16            return True
17        return False
```

17. Before we test the new rule we have created, we
     can make a minor change to the server_deploy.
     yml file to make sure it triggers an error for our new
     rule. Open the server_deploy.yml file with your text
     editor and add in the following two lines into the
     file. We are simply creating a new variable, and the
     aws_secret_access_key provided is a fake key:

```
8
9   var:
10      aws_secret_access_key: AKIAJL123456789qazw
```

18. We can now run our new test as we did earlier with
     the following command. As you can see from the
     output, it should pick up we have hard-coded an
     AWS secret key as part of our playbook:

```
ansible-lint server_deploy.yml -r test_rules/

...

[ANSWERS02] Playbook May Contain AWS Credentials
```

server_deploy.yml:9
    aws_secret_access_key: AGSJDFKSHDGD122343

You can skip specific rules or tags by adding them to your configuration file:

```
# .ansible-lint
warn_list:  # or 'skip_list' to silence them completely
  - 'ANSWERS01'  # Line too long (95 characters)
  - 'ANSWERS02'  # Playbook May Contain AWS Credentials
```

List Ansible Tasks

Another useful command you can use before you deploy your changes out into your working environments and systems is to use the **--list-tasks** option. Just as its name suggests, it will list all of the tasks the playbook is going to run as part of the configuration deployment:

1. Use the **--list-tasks** option over our **server_deploy. yml** playbook to see what tasks are going to be performed as part of running the playbook. Run the following ansible-playbook command, and you should be provided with a list of tasks that will be run:

    ansible-playbook -i hosts server_deploy.yml --list-tasks --ask-vault-pass

    Vault password:

    ```
    playbook: server_deploy.yml
      play #1 (localhost): localhost            TAGS: []
        tasks:
    ```

```
splunk_server : Create the host security group
splunk_server : launch the new ec2 instance
splunk_server : wait for SSH to come up
splunk_server : add tag to instance        TAGS: []
splunk_server : wait for service to be up and
complete        TAGS: []
debug           TAGS: []
splunk_server : create ami for new Splunk
servers         TAGS: []
```

Ansible Check Mode

This can be less useful as some tasks do rely on the output of other tasks to be able to complete, but the **--check** option running as part of your Ansible playbook can give you an insight as to what will be run as part of your plays.

The **--check** option will not make any changes to your remote systems, but if the modules you are using in your playbooks support "check mode," you will get a report on what changes would have been made:

1. Run the following playbook command from your working environment including the --check option, which looks like the playbook is being performed but is not. As you can see, the third task failed as there is no attribute that would be provided after the instance is created in the previous step:

    ansible-playbook -i hosts
    server_deploy.yml --check   --ask-vault-pass

Vault password:

PLAY [localhost] ***********************************

TASK [splunk_server : Create the host security group] ****
ok: [localhost]

TASK [splunk_server : launch the new ec2 instance] *******
skipping: [localhost]

TASK [splunk_server : wait for SSH to come up] ***********
fatal: [localhost]: FAILED! => {"msg": "'dict object' has no attribute 'instances'"}
to retry, use: --limit @/home/vince/Projects/ansible-work/chapter7/server_deploy.retry

PLAY RECAP ***
localhost:
ok=1   changed=0   unreachable=0   failed=1

2. To stop this error from being performed when we run the --check option, we can add the **check_mode:no** into the task being run. We can perform this change now, so open the **roles/server_cloud/tasks/main.yml** with your text editor to add this to our role tasks.

3. Add in the **check_mode** option as part of the
    cloudformation module task being run as we have
    highlighted in the following tasks:

```
 1 ---
 2 - name: start splunk cloudformation stack
 3   cloudformation:
 4     stack_name: "ProdSplunkStack"
 5     state: "present"
 6     region: "{{ aws_region }}"
 7     template: "roles/splunk_cloud/files/splunk-
       stack.yml"
 8     template_parameters:
 9       KeyName: "{{ aws_keypair }}"
10       InstanceType: "{{ aws_instance_type }}"
11       SSHLocation: "{{ aws_ssh_location }}"
12       AWSAMI: "{{ aws_image }}"
13     check_mode: no
14     tags:
15       env: "Production"
16       service: "Splunk"
17   register: production_splunk_stack
```

4. Run the playbook command again including
    the --check option, and hopefully this time, the
    output should no longer provide any failed results:

```
ansible-playbook -i hosts server
_deploy.yml  --check --ask-vault-pass
Vault password:

PLAY [localhost] ***********************************
```

```
TASK [splunk_server : Create the host security
group] ****
ok: [localhost]

TASK [splunk_server : launch the new ec2
instance] *******
skipping: [localhost]

TASK [splunk_server : wait for SSH to come up]
***********
fatal: [localhost]: FAILED! => {"msg": "'dict object'
has no attribute 'instances'"}
to retry, use: --limit @/home/vince/Projects/ansible-
work/chapter7/server_deploy.retry

PLAY RECAP *****************************************
localhost:
ok=1    changed=0    unreachable=0    failed=1
```

Ansible Playbook Syntax Check

Although the syntax check is not as in depth as using ansible-lint, the syntax check allows you to run a quick check over your playbooks and is part of the base Ansible installation. You won't have to install anything else like ansible-lint, which may come in handy on systems where this may not be an option.

All you need to do is run your playbook with the **--syntax-check** option, and even though you won't get a lot of information, it will perform a sanity check on your playbooks to make sure there are no issues with syntax:

1. Perform the following command which uses the **--system-check** option. We also use the **-v** option but still get limited output from the command:

```
ansible-playbook -i hosts cloudformation_deploy.yml -
syntax-check -v
Using /etc/ansible/ansible.cfg as config file
playbook: cloudformation_deploy.yml
```

I hope in this short period of time, we have been able to demonstrate how you can troubleshoot your roles and playbooks using some of the lesser-known features of Ansible.

Ansible Connections Without SSH

So far, all of the times we have been running our Ansible code, we've been using connections using SSH. This is probably the main way you would use Ansible, running configuration management over remote servers in your network.

Ansible does have the option to connect with systems, without using SSH. This is where the ansible_connection option is provided to the user to connect to hosts without using SSH. The following is a list of some of the more commonly used connection types:

- **local** – This is the most common ansible_connection to use at it allows you to deploy to the control machine you are working on.

- **docker** – This will deploy your Ansible code directly into a Docker container using the local Docker client running on your system.

- **winrm** – This is used for Windows hosts, but does need some extra dependencies to help you connect and run your code. The pywinrm package needs to be installed onto your system to allow you to run the connection.

- **vmware_tools** – This is used to run tasks in a guest operating system running in VMware infrastructure.

Note   At the time of writing, there were twenty-six official connections available in Ansible. A full list of all these connection types can be found at the following link: **https://docs.ansible.com/ansible/2.10/plugins/connection.html**.

The most common way to connect with these other types of servers is by adding in extra variables into your inventory file to specify how the connection will work. As well as the connection type being used, you usually need to specify the hostname, user to connect with, and a password to connect with.

In the following section, we will discuss how to use the hosts file to outline these options and use them with our Ansible commands. Earlier in this chapter, we made a change to our hosts file to add extra details to allow Ansible to connect to AWS servers. In this section, we will do something similar to allow you to make non-SSH connections.

Our first example is to set up a hosts file to use a local connection, by using the ansible_connection option as described here:

```
1 [local]
2 localhost ansible_connection=local
3
```

That's all there is to it. If your server does not have SSH running, it will still be able to perform Ansible commands as it does not need to connect to the localhost via SSH. You do need to be working on that machine at the time though. In the following, our next example is for a Docker connection. In this example, we have added a separate vars section for our configuration to specify the host and user to access. There are also the ansible_docker_extra_args options available to provide extra arguments if needed:

```
1 [docker]
2 <docker_container_ip_address>
3 [docker:vars]
4 ansible_connection=docker
7 ansible_user=root
```

As we mentioned earlier, for winrm connections to connect to a Windows host, you first need to have the pywinrm module installed. The connection details you then need to set up specific for winrm are listed as follows including the user to connect with, a password, and if a certificate validation is needed:

```
[win]
192.9.12.122
[win:vars]
ansible_connection=winrm
ansible_user=administrator
ansible_password=<password>
ansible_winrm_server_cert_validation=ignore
```

As a final example, you can see in the following that a configuration for a vmware_tools connection type is very similar to the winrm configuration:

```
[vmware_host]
192.9.12.122
[vmware_host:vars]
ansible_connection: vmware_tools
ansible_vmware_host: vcenter.example.com
```

```
ansible_vmware_user: administrator@vsphere.local
ansible_vmware_password: <password>
ansible_vmware_validate_certs: no
```

Hopefully, this has given you some guidance on how to implement Ansible without needing to use SSH. In our last chapter, we will spend a lot more time looking at the hosts file and how to use different variables and configuration options available.

Migrating to Ansible

Before we finish this chapter, we wanted to spend a short amount of time discussing how you might approach migrating existing configuration management systems to Ansible. After reviewing your current configuration management, you may decide the cost may outweigh the benefit of the migration, especially if your support team is reluctant to learn a new process or support something different.

The first step you may want to look at is doing a proof of concept with your existing environment to see how difficult it may be to move your existing configuration management over to Ansible. This could mean taking a two- or four-week period of time and seeing if it is viable to mirror an existing part of your configuration management onto Ansible.

As part of this proof of concept, work would also include upskilling part of your team to make sure they are part of this. This may include providing dedicated training as well as allowing these team members to commence the migration as part of this process. It can give any team members that may be reluctant or against this migration to gain first-hand experience of why this change will be beneficial.

It may also be tempting to use an automated process or script to migrate your configuration management, but this will not speed things up as correcting any errors may take more time in the long run. As we have learned previously, there are options like Ansible Galaxy to help speed up progress and reduce the time for your migration.

Make sure you look at the type of servers you are wanting to set up. It may be working to set up a common_server that is consistent across all your servers and then, on top of this, have a separate dedicated role for the service your infrastructure is then performing, such as web_server or splunk_server as we have shown previously.

In this book, I hope we have been able to give you an indication of how beneficial Ansible can be, but we need to warn you any migration from an existing configuration management system will not be easy even if you are moving to Ansible.

Summary

In this chapter, we have covered a lot of interesting topics as well as tied up some loose ends in our project. We started off with a discussion on why we need to use specific modules for AWS and looked at ways to work around this. We then looked at working with the debug module and using variables, registered variables, and working with Ansible facts. We then set up our environment to use ansible-lint to test our playbooks while also starting to create our own tests to incorporate into our configuration management to ensure we are working to best practices.

We then went through some of the more unknown options and modules we can use to help ensure our code is up to standard. This included start-at, step, list tasks, check mode, syntax check, and diff, all of which are in place to make our life a little easier at the end of the day.

In our next chapter, we are going to take some time to set up a testing framework using Molecule to help us make sure we are reducing the errors in our code, and we will then start to look at Testinfra to then perform tests on our deployed infrastructure to make sure everything has run successfully.

CHAPTER 8

Testing Ansible with Molecule

In the previous chapter, we started looking at ways to test and troubleshoot your Ansible code using different options provided by Ansible like --step, ansible-lint, and --syntax-check. In this chapter, we are going to take this testing further by installing and using the Molecule application, which will allow us to use it as a testing framework over our Ansible roles and playbooks.

We have dedicated the entire chapter to using Molecule as there is a lot of work we will need to cover. In this chapter

- We will introduce you to Molecule, explaining what it is, how you can use it to test your Ansible code and install it onto your system.

- Then, we will use Molecule to commence testing our Ansible roles, using a simple example to help you get used to how it works.

- We will then extend our knowledge further by testing our Splunk server role as well.

- We will then show you how to integrate infrastructure testing into Molecule to help you verify the end product of your configuration management is correct and working as you want it to.

V. Sesto, *Practical Ansible*, https://doi.org/10.1007/978-1-4842-8643-2_8

- Finally, we will introduce you to automated testing and deployments and how to use Molecule with an application like Travis CI.

If this is all new to you, don't worry, we will explain everything we do, but it should provide you with the tools to then implement testing into your code on future projects.

Ansible Testing with the Molecule Testing Framework

Molecule is a testing framework built specifically to test Ansible roles and playbooks and will include some of the features already discussed in our previous chapter.

The aim of Molecule is to test your Ansible roles and playbooks in isolation as it launches a Docker image to run your playbook and then performs tests over it. You can then run your playbook over different instance types and versions to verify it still runs, with Molecule also having the additional feature of being able to run Testinfra tests.

Once it verifies that the role ran successfully, it then cleans everything up and removes all the Docker images used to create your testing environment.

Molecule is Python based and requires docker-py as part of the install as this is how it will interface with Docker. Molecule is currently supported by Red Hat and comes with a suite of tools to help you create a testing workflow for your Ansible code. Since the first edition of this book, Red Hat has invested a lot into Molecule, and there has been a lot of progress and changes in the way it works. The main flow of commands you will use within your work will revolve around the following Molecule commands:

- **molecule init** – This command initializes our existing role, and if needed, we can create a new role from scratch the same as we used the ansible-galaxy command in our earlier chapters. As well as creating the default directories, the molecule init command will also create the default Molecule configuration files.

- **molecule create** – The create command sets up and prepares a provisioner for the Ansible role to be tested against. This will download and create a Docker image that has been provided in the Molecule configuration and will install any required applications if needed. We can provision numerous instances, including different operating systems and version of operating systems if needed.

- **molecule list** – We can get a list of the provisioned instances set up and if they have been successfully tested.

- **molecule converge** – One of the default files created as part of the initialization is the converge.yml file. This file is a playbook created to run your role from start to finish. This can be modified if needed but is a good place to start if you have never used Molecule before.

- **molecule test** – The test command runs through the entire set of default Molecule commands. It will

  - Perform syntax checks and linting over your code.

  - Make sure there are no instances running.

  - Prepare a clean test instance.

  - Run your converge playbook.

- Verify everything is working as planned.

- Then clean everything up afterward.

The first four commands presented earlier provide the user with a way of creating and testing their playbooks and roles with the molecule test command being provided to perform a complete end-to-end test of the user roles and can be easily included in a continuous integration platform like Jenkins or TravisCI.

Note If you do not have Docker installed in your system, you will need to have this installed before you move on with the exercises in this section of the book. Go to the following domain if you need more information on how to install and run Docker on your system:

`https://docs.docker.com/engine/install/ubuntu/`

In the following part of this chapter, we will install Molecule and create a new role to demonstrate how to use it. If you're not back in your working environment, log back in to perform the following work:

1. To install **Molecule** on your system, we use the **pip3** command to install the application. As part of the install, also use the docker option to ensure docker-py is installed:

   ```
   pip3 install molecule[docker]
   ```

2. Once the installation is complete, we can verify Molecule is installed by running the **molecule** command with the **--version** option:

   molecule --version

   ```
   molecule 3.6.1 using python 3.7
       ansible:2.10.17
   ```

```
delegated:3.6.1 from molecule
docker:1.1.0 from molecule_docker requiring
collections:
community.docker>=1.9.1
```

3. Molecule can work in a similar way to the ansible-
    galaxy command in setting up our Ansible roles,
    so we will test this functionality out. Move into the
    roles directory so we can then create a new test role:

    cd roles/

4. To create a new role, we use the **molecule** command
    with the **init** option. Run the following command
    to create a new role called test_role. As Molecule
    is closely integrated with ansible-galaxy now, you
    also need to include a namespace or your Galaxy
    account before the role name. Also include the
    driver we want to use as docker:

    ```
    molecule init role vincesesto.test_role -d docker

    INFO     Initializing new role test_role...
    No config file found; using defaults
    - Role test_role was created successfully
    [WARNING]: No inventory was parsed, only implicit
    localhost is available
    localhost | CHANGED => {"backup": "","changed":
    true,"msg": "line added"}
    INFO     Initialized role in roles/test_role
    successfully.
    ```

The preceding command has used vincesesto as the namespace for Galaxy, but make sure you use your own account name.

Note   If you have an existing role you would like to start testing with Molecule, you can still use the init option, but you need to be inside the role directory and then run the command **molecule init scenario** to add all the relevant directories and structure to the existing role.

---

5. The init command will set up your role directory structure for the new role. If you perform the **tree** command on the test_role directory, you will see an output similar to the one we have provided. You will notice all the directories have been set up for us, but compared to our normal ansible-galaxy roles, we also have a **molecule** directory that has been created, specifically for the Molecule configurations:

```
tree test_role/
test_role/
├── defaults
│   └── main.yml
├── files
├── handlers
│   └── main.yml
├── meta
│   └── main.yml
├── molecule
│   └── default
│       ├── converge.yml
│       ├── molecule.yml
```

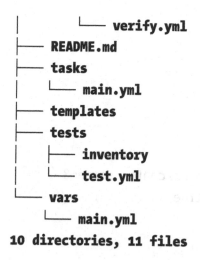

```
|           └── verify.yml
├── README.md
├── tasks
│   └── main.yml
├── templates
├── tests
│   ├── inventory
│   └── test.yml
└── vars
    └── main.yml
10 directories, 11 files
```

6. Molecule has six files created in the default
    directory. The molecule.yml includes all the
    configurations; the coverage.yml and verify.yml are
    basically Ansible playbooks to run the role we have
    created. For now, open the **test_role/molecule/**
    defaults/molecule.yml file with your text editor.

7. As you can see, the configuration files are fairly
    clear. Dependencies are handled by Ansible Galaxy,
    the driver to provision instances is Docker, and we
    have one platform currently set up. If you move to
    the middle of the file, the platforms section specifies
    the image we use for testing. Change the name of
    the platform to something we will recognize when
    we run the tests; in our example, we have used the
    name **test_role**:

```
---
dependency:
  name: galaxy
driver:
  name: docker
platforms:
  - name: test_role
    image: quay.io/centos/centos:stream8
    pre_build_image: true
provisioner:
  name: ansible
verifier:
  name: ansible
```

8. The first thing we can do with Molecule is to run
    the **molecule create** command. This will set up
    the provisioners for our tests to be run across, but
    we first need to be in the role directory to allow the
    applications to find the configurations it needs. Start
    by moving into the new test_role directory:

    cd test_role

9. Before we run the create command, we need to
    make sure the community.docker galaxy playbooks
    are installed onto our system. I am not sure why this
    needs to be installed as it should be installed when
    you install Molecule, so you may already have this
    depending on what version of Molecule you are
    running:

    ansible-galaxy collection install community.docker

10. Run the **molecule create** command which will
     prepare the Docker instance ready for testing to
     commence. You will see a large output similar
     to a playbook running, and we have removed
     most of the following output, with the final line
     showing "**Skipping, prepare playbook not
     configured.**" A prepare.yml file can be placed in our
     molecule/default directory if we need to add extra
     requirements before running the tests:

molecule create

```
INFO     default scenario test matrix: dependency,
         create, prepare
INFO     Performing prerun...
...
order to enable Ansible to find the role using its
expected full name.
INFO     Running default > dependency
WARNING  Skipping, missing the requirements file.
WARNING  Skipping, missing the requirements file.
INFO     Running default > create
INFO     Sanity checks: 'docker'
...

PLAY RECAP *******************************************
localhost                  :
ok=5     changed=2     unreachable=0     failed=0
skipped=4     rescued=0     ignored=0

INFO     Running default > prepare
WARNING  Skipping, prepare playbook not configured.
```

Note   The Molecule documentation recommends you only use Docker as your driver to test your Ansible code on. By doing this, you are reducing the complexity of the platforms you are deploying to and are ensuring your testing is running as quickly as possible. There is documentation available to use other drivers if you need to such as vagrant.

11.   We should have our provisioner running, which in our instance is a Docker image. Molecule provides us with a way to check our instances are available with the **molecule list** command. Run this command now to verify you have a provisioner ready with the instance name matching the one you specified in the **molecule.yml** file:

molecule list

```
INFO     Running default > list
Instance Name  Driver Name  Provisioner Name
Scenario Name  Created
---------------------------------------------------------
    test_role    | docker    | ansible           |
    default      | true      | false
```

12.   Our new role doesn't have any tasks to really test yet, so before we move any further, we should create a simple task first. Open the **tasks/main.yml** file and add the following code which uses the **package** module to install **Git** into our image:

```
1 ---
2 - name: Install git
3   package:
4     name: git
5     state: present
```

13. Molecule sets up the **converge.yml** file when we created the role with the molecule init command. This file is a playbook set up to run the role over the provisioned image. We can now use the **molecule converge** command that will run this specific playbook for us, with the role hopefully completing successfully:

molecule converge

```
PLAY [Converge] **********************************

TASK [Gathering Facts] ***************************
ok: [instance]

TASK [Include vincesesto.test_role] **************

TASK [vincesesto.test_role : install git] ********
changed: [instance]

PLAY RECAP ***************************************
instance                  : ok=2
changed=1    unreachable=0    failed=0
skipped=0    rescued=0    ignored=0
```

Note   Molecule also gives us an easy way to troubleshoot issues with our testing. We can use the **molecule login** command in the command line to log directly into the image that has been provisioned to perform the testing on.

---

14. This is great, but we can do more to expand our testing of our new role. Currently, our configuration for Molecule is set up to use Ansible as the verifier. This means it will simply run our role to verify it has been successful; instead, we can create software tests using **Testinfra** to gain extra functionality in our testing. Before we start creating our tests, we need to install the Testinfra package onto our system with the following pip3 command:

    ```
    pip3 install pytest-testinfra
    ```

15. Open the **molecule/default/molecule.yml** file again with your text editor to make a further change.

16. This time, move to the bottom of the file and change the last line from being **ansible** to now being **testinfra** as the verifier:

    ```
    1 ---
    2 dependency:
    3   name: galaxy
    4 driver:
    5   name: docker
    6 platforms:
    7   - name: test_role
    8     image: quay.io/centos/centos:stream8
    9     pre_build_image: true
    ```

266

```
10 provisioner:
11   name: ansible
12 verifier:
13   name: testinfra
```

17. Create a directory for our tests to reside in. Create
the directory named tests in the **molecule/default**
directory with the following command:

mkdir molecule/default/tests

18. Create a file in the new directory you created, which
will hold our Testinfra code. Create and name the
file **test_default.py** using the following command:

touch molecule/default/tests/test_default.py

19. Open the **molecule/default/tests/test_default.**
py file with your text editor. Add in the first four
lines of the following code. Lines 1–3 import all the
necessary Python modules needed by the script,
including the **testinfra** module we installed at the
start of this exercise:

```
1 import os
2
3 import testinfra.utils.ansible_runner
4
```

20. The following lines of code will then be added to the
     file to provide Testinfra with a list of hosts to run the
     tests over:

```
5 testinfra_hosts = testinfra.utils.ansible_runner.
  AnsibleRunner(
6     os.environ['MOLECULE_INVENTORY_FILE']).get_
      hosts('all')
7
```

21. Now add in two test functions that will be run as
     part of our Molecule tests. The first named **test_user**
     will look for the username named root and verify it
     exists. The second function will verify the package
     named **git** is installed. Make sure you have this code
     added to your file ready for the tests to be run:

```
 8 def test_user(host):
 9     user = host.user("root")
10     assert user.exists
11
12 def test_git_is_installed(host):
13     git = host.package("git")
14     assert git.is_installed
```

22. It's time to run the molecule test command.
     As mentioned earlier, this is the entire suite of
     commands across our role:

molecule test

**INFO   default scenario test matrix: dependency, lint,
cleanup, destroy, syntax, create, prepare, converge,
idempotence, side_effect, verify, cleanup, destroy**

...

INFO   Executing Testinfra tests found in /home/ec2-user/practical_ansible_ed2/chapter_8/splunk_server/roles/test_role/molecule/default/tests/

...

The output will be large, and if we follow it from start to finish, we should get to a point where it runs the Action: **'verify'. This is where all the tests in the molecule/default/tests** directory are run over the provisioned Docker images once the Ansible roles have been completed. As you can see in the following, the output provides details of the tests run and which have successfully completed:

```
=========== test session starts ===========
platform linux -- Python 3.7.10, pytest-7.1.2,
pluggy-1.0.0
rootdir: /
plugins: testinfra-6.7.0, testinfra-6.0.0
collected 2 items

molecule/default/tests/test_default.py ..
[100%]

=========== 2 passed in 6.55s ===========
INFO      Verifier completed successfully.
...
```

I hope in this short period of time, we have been able to demonstrate how you can test your roles and playbooks using Molecule and add extra testing capabilities with Testinfra. In the next section, we are going to take a closer look at using Molecule within AWS, and with that, we can look at implementing testing for our Splunk server running in the cloud.

Using Molecule with Code Deployed to AWS

The work we have done in this chapter is perfect for testing our configuration that is running on a stand-alone server as we can use a Docker image that mirrors the server we are installing onto and make sure everything works before we implement the change further.

But what about the servers we have been running on AWS? If we try to run the same Ansible code on a Docker container, nothing will really work as all the modules we are using relate to AWS. We could change our code to fit our Docker container, but this would then change the code and would not be relevant for our AWS environments.

What we want to be able to do is test the code and then deploy the code without any changes.

Molecule originally was developed with a long list of drivers that would cater for your needs. To simplify this, the base installation of Molecule is now limited but allows other community drivers to be installed separately, just as we are about to do shortly. The Ansible community supports an EC2 driver that can be used to work with and test your AWS Ansible modules.

As part of the Ansible EC2 modules, you would have needed to install boto to make sure Ansible can interface with AWS; this is also required for Molecule to work with AWS.

Previously, we used the molecule init role command to create a new role from scratch. We don't need to do that with an existing role. Instead, we can use the molecule init scenario command to make use of the existing Splunk server role we have been working on. We can work on this now to demonstrate how this work, so log back into your working environment and we will get started:

1. Just in case you are working on a new environment
    and have not had the boto, boto3, or awscli packages
    installed, run the following pip3 command to verify
    they are all installed and available on your system:

    pip3 install boto boto3 awscli

2. To reduce the complexity of the Molecule code base,
    the EC2 driver needs to be installed separately.
    Use pip3 again to do another installation of the
    molecule-ec2 Python module that we can use as
    part of Molecule:

    pip3 install molecule-ec2

3. We want to set up Molecule in our splunk_server
    role. Because the role is already set up, we need
    to move into the role directory we have previously
    created:

    cd roles/splunk_server/

4. Run the following command which will set
    up the Molecule configurations in the existing
    splunk_server role this time using the init scenario
    command options:

    ```
    molecule init scenario -d ec2
    INFO     Initializing new scenario default...
    INFO     Initialized scenario in roles/splunk_server/
             molecule/default successfully.
    ```

5. When using scenario, we do not provide a name
    to the role as it already comes with one. We did
    not give it a valid namespace though when we did
    create it, so update the meta/main.yml file to make

sure you have a valid namespace. Open the file with your text editor and make sure the first four lines are filled in with valid details:

```
1 galaxy_info:
2   author: vincesesto
3   description: fully loaded splunk server
4   company: your company (optional)
```

6. If we use the tree command over our splunk_server role, we can now see the extra directories and configurations that have been created for Molecule. In the following output, we are only showing the files in the molecule directory created with our new Molecule scenario:

```
tree splunk_server/molecule/
splunk_server/molecule/
└── default
    ├── converge.yml
    ├── create.yml
    ├── destroy.yml
    ├── INSTALL.rst
    ├── molecule.yml
    ├── prepare.yml
    └── verify.yml
```

```
1 directory, 7 files
```

Everything will look similar to the previous Molecule scenario we created earlier, but as part of the ec2 driver, we should also see a create.yml and destroy.yml playbook.

7. If we open the molecule.yml, you will notice the
    driver is now ec2. But you will need to add in the
    platform details to match the instance values you
    want to use. In the following, we are adding in the
    image_owner, image_name, instance_type, and the
    vpc_subnet_id for our AWS account:

```
1    ---
2    dependency:
3      name: galaxy
4    driver:
5      name: ec2
6    platforms:
7      - name: instance
8        image_owner: "137112412989"
9        image_name: amzn2-ami-kernel-5.10-
           hvm-2.0.20220426.0-x86_64-gp2
10       instance_type: t2.micro
11       vpc_subnet_id: subnet-<your_account_vpc>
12       tags:
13         Name: molecule_instance
14   provisioner:
15     name: ansible
16   verifier:
17     name: ansible
```

8. Lines 8 and 9 should be available for some time
    now, so feel free to use the same values for your
    molecule.yml file. You will need to get the vpc_
    subnet_id value from your AWS account. To get the
    correct vpc_subnet_id, we can use the following
    command to get the correct subnet for our AWS

environment. You will get an output similar to the
one shown in the following, where you need to use
one of the values provided as SubnetId:

```
aws ec2 describe-subnets
{
    "Subnets": [
        {
            "MapPublicIpOnLaunch": true,
            "AvailabilityZoneId": "apse2-<removed>.",
            "AvailableIpAddressCount": 4090,
            "DefaultForAz": true,
            "SubnetArn": "arn:aws:ec2:ap-southeast-2:
            removed:subnet/subnet-<removed>",
            "Ipv6CidrBlockAssociationSet": [],
            "VpcId": "vpc-26923842",
            "MapCustomerOwnedIpOnLaunch": false,
            "AvailabilityZone": "ap-southeast-2b",
            "SubnetId": "subnet-<removed>",
            "OwnerId": "<removed>",
            "CidrBlock": "172.31.32.0/20",
            "State": "available",
            "AssignIpv6AddressOnCreation": false
        },
```

9. Create our ec2 instance with Molecule just as we
   did when we were working with Docker using the
   create command. As the EC2 instance will take
   a little longer than a Docker container, you will
   need to allow an extra minute or two for the create
   command to complete:

```
molecule create
```

10. You can log into your AWS web console and see
    if am EC2 is created. As you can see in Figure 8-1,
    we can see the image named molecule_instance,
    the same as what we have tagged in our
    configuration file.

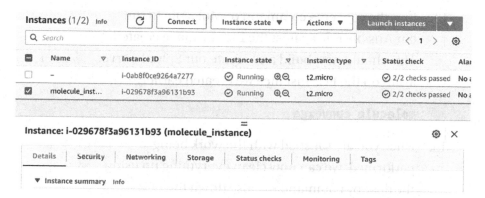

Figure 8-1. *The AWS Web Console Showing Our Molecule Test*
Instance.

11. Specific to our testing, when we created our
    original Ansible playbook, we encrypted all of our
    variables with ansible-vault. We will need to set up a
    password file that Molecule will be able to read and
    use. Once again, open the molecule.yml file with
    your text editor and move to the bottom of the file
    and add in the config_options as we have including
    the location for the vault_password_file:

```
14 provisioner:
15   name: ansible
16   config_options:
17   defaults:
18     vault_password_file: ~/.ansible-vault-
       password-file.txt
```

275

12. Create the vault password file in your home directory, making sure it is the same name as the previous file. And make sure you add in your password that you have previously used to run the Ansible playbook.

13. Run the converge command of Molecule to run our Ansible role against the EC2 instance created. This should now build and create our Splunk server again on the EC2 instance we created earlier:

```
molecule converge
```

14. Once you are satisfied with the work being performed, we can now clean everything up using the destroy command to close down the EC2 instance being used by Molecule:

```
molecule destroy
```

We are almost there. All that is needed is some tests to run over our infrastructure to verify everything has been set up correctly. In the next section of this chapter, we will use Testinfra like we did with our Docker image to test and verify that everything has been set up and our infrastructure is running as it should.

Update Tests to Match Our AWS Instance

This is some good progress to now allow our Splunk server to start up and run in AWS as part of our Molecule testing. This goes a long way in allowing us to verify any production changes should not fail, but we currently don't have any relevant tests to run over our server. In the next section of this chapter, we will add tests to verify the components of our server are set up correctly and can be tested with Molecule.

Before we move on though, why do we need to use an application like Testinfra, which allows us to create unit tests to test the actual state of our servers' configurations? So far, our configurations have been relatively simple, even with our Splunk server role. But as things improve and the complexity increases, an automated way to test the state of our actual configurations becomes more necessary. These tests serve a number of purposes, the first being that they almost act like an extra form of documentation where someone new to the environment can look through the tests and see what is important on this specific server. Secondly, if we set up our testing using an application like Testinfra, it then allows us to automate the process of testing when changes are made to our code.

For our Splunk server project, I think it will be a good start to at least test for the Splunk application being installed on our server and to make sure it is running and accessible from the Internet. As well we can also test to verify our test Splunk App is installed. This should give you some first-hand knowledge in setting up tests for your infrastructure and show you how easy it really is.

Note   Testinfra was created as a plugin to the commonly used test framework Pytest. All of the assertions and tests we are performing in the following can be found in the Pytest documentation at this location: **https://docs.pytest.org/en/7.1.x/**.

To do this, we will need to access our working environment again and make some changes to the Molecule code:

1. As we did with our Docker testing, we created a directory for our tests in the molecule/defaults directory. Start by doing this with the following command:

```
mkdir molecule/default/tests/
```

2. Create the tests_default.py file in the directory
    we have just created so we can start creating our
    infrastructure tests:

```
touch molecule/default/tests/test_default.py
```

3. The process of adding in our tests is similar to
    when we added them to the test role we created
    earlier in this chapter. We need to start by adding
    in the modules we want to use in our testing. The
    os module will allow our test to interface with the
    operating system, the testinfra.util.ansible_runner
    will perform the testing as part of Ansible, and the
    urllib2 module will be able to connect to the web
    interface to make sure Splunk is running on the
    Internet. Open the file with your text editor and add
    in the following code to the start of the file:

```
1    import os
2    import testinfra.utils.ansible_runner
3    import urllib2
```

4. Move down a line or two and we will then load the
    host values for your Splunk server so it will be able
    to connect and start testing:

```
5    testinfra_hosts = testinfra.utils.ansible_runner.
     AnsibleRunner(os.environ['MOLECULE_INVENTORY_
     FILE']).get_hosts('splunk_server')
```

5. Move down a line and we can add in our first test.
    The following code tests to see if the Splunk service
    is running on the EC2 instance we are testing on.

The assert value in the last line of the function will
return if the service is running or not:

```
7   def test_splunk_service_is_running(host):
8       splunk_service = host.service('splunk')
9       assert splunk_service.is_running
```

6. We have just verified the Splunk service is running
   on the server; for our next test, we can verify if
   the web interface is also accessible, meaning our
   ports are open correctly and the Splunk service is
   configured correctly to provide pages to users:

```
11 def test_splunk_is_accessible_on_port_8000(host):
12     host_ip = host.interface("eth0").addresses[0]
13     response = urllib2.urlopen(ip+':8000')
14     assert len(response.read()) > 0
```

The second line of the function creates a variable
named host_ip and gets the IP address assigned to
the EC2 instance. It then uses the urllib2 module
to test if the Splunk web page is accessible on
port 8000.

7. In the last test, we will verify that the Test Splunk
   App we installed using ansible-pull is also installed.
   This is a simple test to verify the directory for the
   app has been created and is in the correct location.

```
16 def test_splunk_apps_are_installed(host):
17     app_dir = host.file('/opt/splunk/etc/apps/
       ansible_test_app')
18     assert app_dir.exists
19     assert app_dir.contains('Test App Installed')
```

8. Save the details in the test_default.py file ready for
    us to run our tests over our infrastructure.

9. We can now run molecule test to create, run, test,
    and clean up afterward:

```
molecule test
```

Note   If you run molecule test and see an error suggesting your
AWS region has not been specified, you may need to export the
region as an environment variable as some of the versions of
Molecule do not pick up AWS configurations correctly.

Finally, our work is done and we can hopefully verify that any changes
made to our Ansible code will deploy without causing any major issues
to environment. This still leaves us with having to perform these changes
manually every time we make a change to test our code. In the following
section, we will use TravisCI to automate the process and provide a visual
interface on the work to allow others to collaborate and work together as
part of our changes, testing, and deployment of our configuration code.

CICD with TravisCI

Our work in this chapter has allowed us to create a testing procedure we
can run every time we make a change to the configuration code. This is
a great first step, and working on your own, this is a perfect way to test as
you make changes. If you are working in a team, this is probably not the
best way to approach your daily work. If you have worked with a team of
developers before, each team will have a standard way of working where
each change, feature, or bug has a ticket assigned to it, the tickets are
taken, and the developer will then grab the specific code from the team's

code repository, create a branch for the work, make the changes, and possibly test on their own laptop or PC, before committing their changes back into the repository.

Once this code has been committed to the repository, there will usually be an automated process where these changes are then deployed into a development or staging environment, and tests are then run against these changes to verify everything is working as it should.

This shouldn't be any different for our Ansible code we have been working on. So far, we've been testing our code on our own personal systems, and the code has been stored in a central repository; in the case of this book, we are using GitHub. All that is needed to complete this way of working is to have an automated process where our changes are automatically tested and deployed into a development environment.

In this part of the chapter, we are going to use TravisCI as part of our work to set up an automated testing environment whenever we make changes to our code. But why do we need to use an application such as this? An application like TravisCI can allow you to set up a central location where all developers in your team can use the one application to perform automated testing on your code. Even if you are working alone, it allows you to keep track of your historical testing in one location, which can be accessed at any time as long as you have an Internet connection. You can also set up testing to run at a specific time of day or run performance testing on your infrastructure to make sure it will all run correctly even during high load periods.

There are a number of applications that can do exactly what we want including CircleCI, Jenkins, Bamboo, and GitLab. Some of these applications are hosted on the Internet as a service, but some of the others need to be hosted on your own hardware. We have decided to use TravisCI as it is a well-known, web-based, continuous integration platform, and if you have been working along so far, you may have noticed that our ansible-galaxy command not only creates our Ansible role file structure but also creates a default .travis.yml file to get us started using the application.

If you haven't used TravisCI before, don't worry, we will start with some of the basics to get you started before we move further into using our Molecule tests with TravisCI:

1. If you don't have an account with TravisCI, this is probably the best time to get started. It has a 30-day free trial, and from there, you can decide if you want to keep working with the application or not. To get started, go to the following web address for the TravisCI web page:

   www.travis-ci.com/

2. Everything is straightforward as far as creating an account. Once the web page loads, click the "Start Today" button on the top right of the page.

3. We've been using GitHub with our projects, so we will also use the "Sign Up With GitHub" option when creating an account. This means that our repositories on GitHub will be linked to TravisCI as soon as the sign-up process is complete.

4. You will be presented with the option to Authorize TravisCI as shown in Figure 8-2. Click the button to proceed.

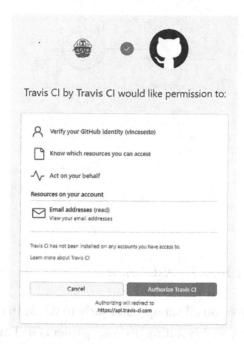

Figure 8-2. *Authorize TravisCI As Part of the Sign-Up Process.*

5. You will also need to confirm email as part of the
    activation process, so do this to proceed.

6. You will also be presented with an option to
    "activate Your GitHub Repositories." This will allow
    all your repositories to be available on TravisCI as
    soon as you start.

7. To get started, you will also need to select a plan. As
    we started earlier, click the "Trial Plan" which is free
    for 30 days. You should see an image similar to the
    one in Figure 8-3.

Select Plan

Monthly Plans   Annual Plans

Trial Plan	1 Concurrent plan	2 Concurrent plan	5 Concurrent plan
Free	$69/monthly	$129/monthly	$249/monthly
⊘ 20 concurrent jobs	⊘ 1 concurrent job	⊘ 2 concurrent jobs	⊘ 5 concurrent jobs
⊘ Private & Open-Source repos	⊘ Private & Open-Source repos	⊘ Private & Open-Source repos	⊘ Private & Open-Source repos
⊘ Linux, Windows, macOS, FreeBSD	⊘ Linux, Windows, macOS, FreeBSD	⊘ Linux, Windows, macOS, FreeBSD	⊘ Linux, Windows, macOS, FreeBSD
Select plan	Select plan	Select plan	Select plan
Learn more	Learn more	Learn more	Learn more

Looking for more credits, users or VM sizes? Contact our Sales Team

Figure 8-3. *Select Your TravisCI Plan*

This should have you all set up and ready to work. In the next section, we will get you started with setting up your projects in TravisCI and triggering a build.

One of the main reasons we are using TravisCI is because it integrates so well with Ansible and Molecule. If you may have noticed, whenever we create an Ansible role with ansible-galaxy or Molecule, a file called .travis. yml is created for you as well. If you have not worked with TravisCI before, all you need is the this .travis.yml file in the root file of your repository, and TravisCI will start building your work.

The code for this book is in one giant repository, so the TravisCI will not pick up the configuration file created in each of the roles. Log back into your working environment, and we will quickly run through setting up a new repository and show you how TravisCI will be able to automatically pick up your changes and trigger a build:

1. Log into the GitHub web interface with your user account, and click the top-right plus button to create a new repository; in this instance, call it test_role to set up the work we did earlier in this chapter. If you

would like to see how my code is set up, you can view it at the following link:

https://github.com/vincesesto/test_role

2. Perform a clone of your new repository into your working environment, so you should have a new directory called test_role. Change into that role before copying files across:

cd test_role

3. If you are working along with the code from this book, you can run the following command to copy the existing role into our new GitHub repository:

cp -r practical_ansible_ed2/tree/main/chapter_8/splunk_
server/roles/test_role .

4. Once all the data is in the test_role repository, commit and push your changes to GitHub.

5. As we have set up TravisCI to use our GitHub repositories, and we have a .travis.yml file in our root directory of the new test_role, if you log into the TravisCI web interface, the main dashboard screen should show you that a build has been triggered for the test_role repository.

6. From your dashboard, click the test_role build job and you will be taken to the details page of your build job. It provides a load of useful information and is a good place to start to investigate when things go wrong. The basic configurations for the .travis.yml file will most likely provide you with a build that passes on the first go.

Figure 8-4. *Successfully Complete TravisCI Build*

7.   If we wanted to trigger another build without
     making any changes to our code, we can simply
     click the "More options" button at the top right
     and click "Trigger build," but this should happen
     automatically each time we commit new code to our
     repository.

8.   If we take a closer look at the tasks performed by
     the TravisCI build, you will see it simply does all the
     work outlined in the .travis.yml file. This includes
     installing dependencies, installing Ansible, setting
     up a basic configuration file, and then running the
     following ansible-playbook command:

```
- ansible-playbook tests/test.yml -i
  tests/inventory --syntax-check
```

Note   You may have noticed when you run the ansible-galaxy command, a tests directory is created. Inside this directory is simply a playbook that calls the new role you have just created. At the time of writing, the Ansible documentation has no reference to this directory as to what it needs to be used for and what tests are added here, and this is why we are not using it as part of our work with Molecule.

---

9.   From what we can see, the configuration file does not do any of the work we have set up as part of our Molecule tests. With only a few minor changes to the .travis.yml file, we will be able to have it running Molecule and performing the tests we created earlier. Open the .travis.yml file with your text editor.

10.   We will start by updating the version of Python currently being used. The default file will have the Python version set to 2.7; move to line three of our file and change that to 3.9, which we have been using and have seen that it passes successfully:

```
1  ---
2  language: python
3  python: "3.9"
```

11.   With an update to Python, we also need to update the version of pip3 being installed onto our test environment; in line 12 of our configuration file, change this to python3-pip:

```
9   addons:
10    apt:
11      packages:
12        - python3-pip
```

12.   We also have some extra application that needs to
      be installed before we can start to run Molecule. In
      line 16, change the values to run pip3 and now also
      install version 2.10 of Ansible, Molecule, and the
      pytest-testinfra package. In the line below (i.e., line
      17), you will also need to install the community.
      docker Ansible role from Galaxy:

```
15   # Install applications needed
16   - pip3 install ansible==2.10 molecule[docker]
       pytest-testinfra
17   - ansible-galaxy collection install
       community.docker
```

13.   Instead of checking the version of Ansible being
      installed, we can change this to check the version of
      Molecule. As you might remember, this command
      will also output the version of Ansible and
      supporting Python packages as well:

```
19   # Check ansible version
20   - molecule --version
```

14.   Lastly, move toward the bottom of the file. I prefer
      to keep the syntax check in the file, and a few lines
      down, add in the molecule test command as follows:

```
29   # Perform a molecule test
30   - molecule test
```

15.   Save the changes you have made to the .travis.
      yml file, and in a few seconds, TravisCI will start
      building your Ansible and Molecule code, and in
      a few minutes, you should also have a successfully
      completed build.

In a short period of time, we have been able to move our Ansible code onto an automated, web-based, testing application. TravisCI will run whenever we make a change to our code as well as keep a historical record for future reference. Even though the work we have performed has been straightforward and relatively easy, there is still a lot we have not covered. If you are looking for more detailed information on using TravisCI, they have detailed documentation at the following link: `www.travis-ci.com/ getting-started/`.

Using AWS on TravisCI

We did not want to spend too much time on TravisCI as this was only meant to be a quick introduction, but there is one thing we need to cover before finishing off this chapter. In the previous section, we set up Molecule to work with our splunk_server role on AWS. This can also be performed with TravisCI, but we need to make one minor additional change before proceeding with the build job.

For TravisCI to work with AWS, you will need to provide the web application with your AWS Access keys and Secret keys. Sharing these values in plain text is a major security risk, so to work around this, each TravisCI build job has environment variables you can set in the Settings section of your build job.

Clicking the "More options" button and then selecting "Settings" will present you with settings for your build, including a section available on environment variables. You should see something similar to the image in Figure 8-5, where you will see your AWS configurations stored securely.

Environment Variables

Customize your build using environment variables. For secure tips on generating private keys read our documentation

AWS_ACCESS_KEY	🔒 •••••••••••••••	Available to all branches	🗑
AWS_DEFAULT_REGION	🔒 •••••••••••••••	Available to all branches	🗑
AWS_SECRET_KEY	🔒 •••••••••••••••	Available to all branches	🗑

💬 If your secret variable has special characters like `&`, escape them by adding `\` in front of each special character. For example, `ma&w!doc` would be entered as `ma\&w\!doc`.

NAME	VALUE	BRANCH			
Name	Value	All branches ▾	⊗	DISPLAY VALUE IN BUILD LOG	Add

Figure 8-5. *Setting Environment Variables for TravisCI*

To then use these variables in your .travis.yml file, you will then set up your AWS configurations after you install your support applications like awscli, boto, and boto3. The following is an example of how you can perform this:

```
# configure AWS CLI
- aws configure set aws_access_key_id $AWS_ACCESS_KEY
- aws configure set aws_secret_access_key $AWS_SECRET_KEY
- aws configure set default.region $AWS_DEFAULT_REGION
# show AWS CLI config
- aws sts get-caller-identity
```

For the full .travis.yml file including the working Ansible role, we have set up a separate GitHub repository, which is available at the following link:

```
https://github.com/vincesesto/splunk_server
```

Summary

The subject of automated testing can be pretty in depth and complex. When it comes to testing Ansible roles and playbooks, you could quite easily dedicate an entire book to the subject. I think we have still made some good progress in this chapter though.

In this chapter, we've introduced you to the Molecule testing framework providing you with different details on how it works and how to install the application on your system. We then set up a test project where we were able to create a basic Ansible role using Molecule, and we also created some basic tests using the Testinfra application over a Docker image that can be run and tested on our own system. We then expanded this further by setting up Molecule to start testing an existing Ansible role, specifically running this over AWS. Finally, we introduced you to TravisCI where we were able to set up an account, set up our .travis.yml configuration file, and start performing automated testing through the application.

In the next chapter, we discuss how you can start to manage larger environments where you might be managing a large number of servers using Ansible. This will include a discussion on using Ansible Tower, or the open source version, AWX. Once again, the chapter will have a lot of hands-on, practical work.

CHAPTER 9

Managing Large Server Environments

You have made it to the last chapter of this book. So far, this book has focused a lot on practical real-world examples to help you learn how to use Ansible to manage and configure your technology infrastructure. Although we have done our best to give you real-world examples on how to manage these environments, there is one thing that might be different when you try to implement Ansible into your organization, and this is possibly the number of the hosts and servers you are working with.

Working for a large organization providing a web-based service to their customers like an Internet service provider or an eCommerce website, it is not uncommon to be configuring hundreds and, sometimes, thousands of servers. This is why we have dedicated the final chapter of this book to give you some tools and tricks to help you work with larger server environments. In this chapter

- We will show you how to expand your knowledge on hosts files using different techniques to configure and work with a larger number of servers.

- We will discuss how Ansible is able to work with changing or dynamic inventory, while still allowing you to implement changes across these servers.

© Vincent Sesto 2022
V. Sesto, *Practical Ansible*, https://doi.org/10.1007/978-1-4842-8643-2_9

- Lastly, we will provide you with an introduction to Ansible Tower and show you how to install and run an open source version of the application.

As with a majority of the work in this book, the best way to introduce these new tools and techniques is by providing practical examples, so we will get started straight away.

Managing Inventory and Hosts Files

As we've been working with our projects, our hosts files have increased with the size of our infrastructure, but the number of hosts has only increased to our five or six hosts or IP address. You can imagine that in the real world, you could be using Ansible to implement changes and manage configuration across hundreds or even thousands of servers across different locations or regions. In the second part of this chapter, we will look at using Ansible Tower to help organize and manage your infrastructure, but resorting to an application like Ansible Tower is not needed, even if you are deploying to a large number of hosts.

As you have seen in the previous chapter, Ansible works against multiple servers in our hosts file, where we specify a group of servers. Once these groups have been set up, we can use these groups to run our Ansible module, playbooks, and roles against.

With a little planning and organization, you can expand your hosts files to manage all the inventory you need. In this part of the chapter, we are going to show you some of the functionality of the hosts files that will help you organize and manage your real-world environments.

Note   Don't forget /etc/ansible/hosts is the default location for hosts files, but we have been using the -i option to specify the file we wish to use, allowing us to really use any location for our inventory.

We also use the work hosts and inventory files interchangeably and they are both the same thing. Ansible names your default inventory file as "hosts" and is one of the reasons we use this term as well as inventory.

Using Multiple Hosts Files

When working with a larger number of servers, one of the easiest things to do to help you manage your environment is to use multiple hosts or inventory files as needed. This is especially good if you need to deploy to a development environment and your own laptop at the same time.

As an example, you could create a LocalHosts inventory file for your own laptop, while creating a separate inventory file for the development environment named DevHosts. You could then specify inventory parameters when running your playbook from the command line:

```
ansible-playbook server_play.yml -i LocalHosts -i DevHosts
```

Instead of needing to refer to more than one inventory file as part of your command, another way you could achieve this is by placing all the inventory files you use in one directory and then refer to the directory when using the Ansible command. For example, your directory may be called development_inventory and consist of the two files we mentioned earlier:

```
tree development_inventory/
-- LocalHosts
-- DevHosts
```

We could then specify the directory as part of our command-line command, instead of all the files located in the directory:

```
ansible-playbook server_play.yml -i development_inventory
```

Don't forget, our playbook usually specifies the host that the configurations are deployed to, so we could even add all our inventory into this directory if our playbooks are set up with specific hosts.

Using Ranges in Hosts Files

One way you can minimize the amount of configuration needed with a larger number of servers is by specifying a range in your hosts file. A lot of the time you may need to manage a large number of servers that will all have similar names while only changing the number or letter to specify a difference. By using a range value in square brackets, you can specify a start and end value, separated by a colon.

In the following example, we have our web server domain names, with the only difference in the domain name being the number after the name web. As you can see, we have 50 web serves in our environment and have set up our range of hosts from 01 to 50:

```
[webservers]
web[01:50].example.com
```

Note   Throughout this book, we have been using our host files as INI file format. We can also specify our hosts files as YAML, but I have not found a reason why you would use YAML over INI, but it is something to keep in mind in case you are required to manage configurations set up in YAML format.

Instead, our following database servers are distinguished by letters at the end from "a" to "f":

```
[databases]
db-[a:f].example.com
```

Adding Variables in Hosts Files

In our previous chapter, we used variables in our hosts files to specify how we can communicate with non-SSH hosts. We have previously been specifying most of our variables in our playbooks, but we can specify variables for that group of hosts in the hosts file. As you can see in the following example, we have a group of development servers which have variables set for the ntp_server and proxy server to be used:

```
[development]
host1
host2

[development:vars]
ntp_server=ntp.dev.com
proxy=proxy.dev.com
```

Although this can be a little confusing at times, especially when trying to debug an issue, it can reduce the amount of information in your playbooks. For example, if you are adding in extra statements for each environment you have, using variables in your hosts file may be a better option.

Working with Dynamic Inventory

Especially with the work we have done in the second half of this book, we have been working in a cloud environment where we are continuously creating and removing hosts, resulting in the IP address changing. There could be any number of reasons why your IP addresses might be changing within your environment, and as a result, this could cause issues when using a regular static host file. This is where a dynamic inventory will work for you.

Ansible allows you to configure your dynamic inventory in two main ways: through an inventory plugin or through an inventory script. The preference for Ansible is for you to use one of the many inventory plugins provided, but if you are using a CMDB or other system that can provide your host files for you, a script is still an option available.

Depending on the inventory plugin you are using, you will need to have the supporting code to run the plugin. In the example we are using in the following, we are working with the aws_ec2 plugin which needs python3 and boto3 to work. We have been using both in our previous work, so there should not be any need to install these onto our working system again.

1. Before we start setting up the plugin, we wanted to take one minute to show another handy command. We have been providing a lot of documentation via links to websites. There is also the ansible-doc command-line tool that can provide help and information if you need it. Run the following ansible-doc command to get a listing of all the inventory plugins currently available:

```
ansible-doc -t inventory -l
```

```
advanced_host_list                    Parses a
'host list' with ranges
amazon.aws.aws_ec2                    EC2
inventory source
amazon.aws.aws_rds                        rds
instance source
....
toml
Uses a specific TOML file as an
inventory source
```

```
yaml
Uses a specific YAML file as an
inventory source
```

We have cut the output back as there is a long list. As you can see, we have used the ansible-doc command with the -t option to specify the topic of inventory and then the -l option to provide a list.

2. One of the first options available in the list is the aws_ec2 plugin, which is what we will be implementing now. In your working directory, create a new directory called inventory:

```
mkdir inventory
```

3. Within this directory, we will create a basic configuration file that will include details for the AWS EC2 plugin. For now, create the new configuration file in the directory with the following command:

```
touch inventory/aws_ec2.yaml
```

4. Open the aws_ec2.yaml file with your text editor. You can specify a large amount of information in this directory including your AWS Access and Secret keys, and it also allows you to group your hosts by AWS tags. For now, simply add the following two lines which specify the use of the aws_ec2 inventory plugin:

```
1    ---
2    plugin: amazon.aws.aws_ec2
```

5. We also need to specify in our Ansible configuration
    file that we want to enable, to plug in for AWS. On
    your working environment, you should have an
    Ansible configuration in your user's home directory,
    for example, /home/<user_name>/ansible.cfg.
    If not, you should then be able to update the
    configuration file in /etc/ansible/ansible.cfg. Open
    the file with your text editor. You will need to locate
    the inventory section and make sure the following
    option is either uncommented or added:

```
[inventory]
enable_plugins=aws_ec2
```

6. Just before we run the plugin, we need to export our
    AWS Access and Secret keys and our default AWS
    Region. If you already have an AWS configuration
    set up on the system you are working on, feel free to
    skip this step:

```
export AWS_ACCESS_KEY_ID=<your_access_key>
export AWS_SECRET_ACCESS_KEY=<your_secret_key>
export AWS_DEFAULT_REGION=<your_default_region>
```

7. We can now run the ansible-inventory command
    that will use the inventory plugin specified in your
    configuration file. As you can see from the following
    output, I have only one server running on AWS:

```
ansible-inventory -i inventory --graph

@all:
  |--@aws_ec2:
```

```
|   |--ec2-13-210-39-5.ap-southeast-2.compute.
    amazon.com
|--@ungrouped:
```

8. This is great progress, but how do we now use this as
    part of our playbooks? Like we mentioned though in
    our previous chapters, to work with AWS instances,
    we need to specify the user and SSH private key that
    is used to access the host. This way, Ansible will be
    able to communicate with the server. Open your
    ansible.cfg file again and add in the following lines
    in the default section of our configuration file:

```
remote_user = ec2-user
private_key_file = <ssh_key_file_location>
```

9. You can now use the new dynamic inventory the
    same way you used your hosts file with the -i option
    as we have run our previous playbooks.

A lot of the work we have done so far should not have you needing to
use dynamic inventory, but the option is available if you do find yourself
needing it. That brings us to the end of this section in working with host
files to help you manage larger server environments. In the next section,
we will introduce to you Ansible Tower to help you decide if it is the right
fit for you and possibly your way of working.

Introducing Ansible Tower

Ansible Tower is a web-based user interface that allows users to work
and organize their configuration management through the web interface
instead of using the command line. Although this book has gone a long

way to help you be comfortable in the command line, there are still a lot of users who prefer to use a visual interface instead of using the command line.

If you are not familiar with Ansible Tower, it is the enterprise version of Ansible. It offers a more familiar environment for customers that may be less technical and may lead to quicker acceptance and usage for these less technical users.

Ansible Tower not only provides a graphical user interface, but it also provides security controls through role-based access control, job scheduling, inventory management, real-time job status updates, and technical support, among other features.

Being an enterprise version of Ansible, Ansible Tower requires a license to use the software, but if you are interested in using Ansible Tower or testing it out, there is a trial license that is available, and when this book was published, it was free for 60 days.

Note   We don't want to dwell too long on the licensing and usage of Ansible Tower, as we will be working with the open source version AWX. If you are interested in getting a free trial of Ansible Tower, head to the following link for more information: `www.redhat.com/en/technologies/management/ansible/try-it`.

As we've mentioned previously, we will be installing and using Ansible AWX as part of this chapter to help demonstrate how to use the application and what you should expect if you decide to use Ansible Tower. Ansible AWX is the open source project that Ansible Tower was based on and is freely available.

Unfortunately, Ansible AWX is not officially supported and does not have extensive testing as part of changes, so it may not be suitable for installing as a solution into the enterprise, but once we get started, hopefully, it will give you enough exposure to see if it is the right solution for you.

Note   The version of AWX that we install in this chapter is version 17.1.0, while at the time of writing, the latest version is at 18.0. The newer version of AWX requires you to have a Kubernetes cluster running to install AWX, which is a little beyond the scope of this book, but we feel you should be able to still see the benefit of using AWX and Ansible Tower while using version 17.1.0. Even though the interface has changed a little between versions, the concepts of how you can use Ansible Tower AWX remain the same.

Installing AWX Ansible Tower

The installation of Ansible AWS should not be too complex, and we will work through it in this part of this chapter. It comes with its own playbook that will set up a series of Docker images to run AWX on. The installation includes a redis host for caching, a postgres database, and the AWX images, so you will need a little bit of disk space to make sure you can install the services onto your system.

AWX uses a web-based user interface; to access the interface, you will need to have a web browser either on the system you are working on or accessible to your environment.

The documentation for AWX outlines the following system requirements as a minimum for a basic installation:

- 4GB of RAM

- 3.4GHz CPU with at least two cores

- 20GB of disk space

You will also need to make sure you have Ansible installed on your system, Docker needs to be running, and the playbook that installs AWX will also use docker-compose to install and run all of the services on Docker, so you will need to make sure it is also installed onto your system. We will perform an installation as part of this chapter, so log back into your working environment and we will demonstrate how to get it up and running:

1. Use wget to download the 17.1.0 version of AWX onto your system ready to start the installation:

   ```
   sudo wget https://github.com/ansible/awx/
   archive/17.1.0.zip
   ```

2. This will download the 17.1.0.zip package into your working directory. Use the unzip command to extract the zip file in the directory you are working in:

   ```
   sudo unzip 17.1.0.zip
   ```

3. You will need to make some minor changes to the inventory file before running the install playbook for AWX, so move into the installation directory for the AWX application with the following command:

   ```
   cd awx-17.1.0/installer/
   ```

4. Open the inventory file with your text editor, and you will notice it is a large file with a large amount of configuration details. Move down to line 107 where

you will need to set a password for the admin user;
you will also need to make sure there is a secret_key
set at about line 116 for decryption and encryption.
If you are just trialing AWX, feel free to leave this
value as the one specified in the following:

```
107 admin_user=admin
108 admin_password=password
109
110 # Whether or not to create preload data for
    demonstration purposes
111 create_preload_data=True
112
113 # AWX Secret key
114 # It's *very* important that this stay the
    same between upgrades or you will lose the
    ability to decrypt
115 # your credentials
116 secret_key=awxsecret
```

5. Save the inventory file and you can now run the
    install.yml playbook from the installer directory
    with the following command:

```
ansible-playbook -i inventory install.yml
```

The playbook does quite a bit of work including
installing all the Docker images and then installing and
configuring AWX on these images.

6. Once the playbook is complete, the first thing you should do is see the images that have been installed on your host, to specifically see the work the install playbook performs. Do this by running the docker images command as follows:

```
docker images
    REPOSITORY    TAG      IMAGE ID       CREATED      SIZE
    postgres      12       bc02a3fd9d66 6 days ago 373MB
    redis         latest   53aa81e8adfa 6 days ago 117MB
    centos        8        5d0da3dc9764 8 months    231MB
    ansible/awx   17.1.0   599918776cf2 15 months   1.41GB
```

7. Running the docker ps command, you will then be able to see a redis and postgres service running and two AWX services running.

8. You should have a fully functioning version of AWX now running on your system. To access the web interface, open a web browser that is accessible to your system and enter the IP address to your system. You should see a login screen similar to the image in Figure 9-1.

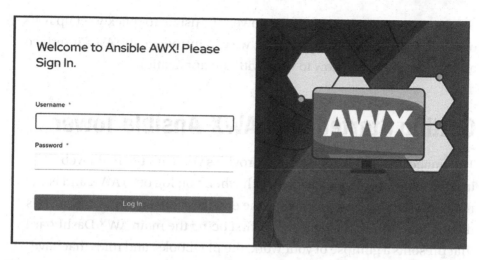

Figure 9-1. The AWX Login Screen Presented Once Installation Is Complete

9. In step four of this exercise, we set the username
    and password for the admin user. Use these
    credentials to log into the web interface, and if all
    has worked, you should now be presented with the
    AWS main dashboard shown in Figure 9-2.

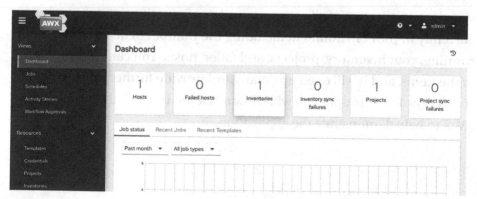

Figure 9-2. The AWX Dashboard Presented Upon Login

Once again, we have used the power of Ansible to quickly set up AWX onto our system. In the next section, we will introduce the AWX interface and start to show you how to work with the application.

Getting Started with AWX Ansible Tower

The image presented in Figure 9-2 provides you with the main web interface page you are presented with when you log onto AWX and is the main interface you use to manage the environment and application. It is divided into two main sections, the first being the main AWX Dashboard that presents a glimpse of your work, the playbooks, and roles that have been run and any up and coming work. The second is the main menu on the right of the page where you then make selections on the part of your work that you need to configure.

Main Dashboard

The main dashboard presented when you log in allows you to monitor the hosts and implement scheduled jobs in your environment. It gives you a visual representation of all your code and configurations and shows hosts currently in your environment including the number of hosts currently running, your inventory, projects, and failed hosts. You can click on each of the items, and it will open up details and provide further information. If you click Projects option, it will show a "Demo Project" that comes with AWX to help demonstrate the application.

Figure 9-3. *The Projects Screen Showing the Default Demo Project Added As Part of the Installation*

The AWX Ansible Tower Main Menu

The main menu on the left side of the screen provides you with all the different configuration options you can make changes to within your environment. If you log into the web interface, you will notice there are five main sections of the main menu which includes views, resources, access, administration, and settings:

- **Views** – This allows you to show different visual information similar to the main dashboard screen. Jobs shows the playbooks that have been run, schedule shows you any scheduled jobs that are planned, and activity stream shows a log of all the combined activities on AWX.

- **Resources** – This is where all your code is represented and of the resources can be edited directly in the interface. The items in the menu should be familiar with you by now and include templates, credentials, projects, inventories, and hosts.

- **Access** – This helps you manage the users who have access to the application and provides you with the ability to define specific access rights to the users. It allows you to define an organization as well as setting up specific teams that you can assign your users to.

- **Administration** – These options allow you to define further credentials as well as notification to application like PagerDuty. You can also set configurations for applications like ServiceNow and Jenkins to integrate with AWX Ansible Tower.

- **Settings** – This section provides you with further ways to manage how AWX Ansible Tower both operates and is presented to the user. It enables simplified login for AWX, including Active Directory and ldap authentication for your company. It allows system-level features and logging settings and provides a way to change how the user interface is set up and how jobs are displayed.

The main menu in the AWX Ansible Tower provides you with all the options you will need to manage your Ansible environment. Although there are some new terms in there, a lot of the options should be intuitive to you and should allow you to get started with minimal issues. In the next section of this chapter, we will work through some of the more common options available in the application.

Set Up Your Organization and Users

AWX Ansible Tower includes a default organization, but you can also add your own organization. Access the organization from the option located on the left navigation bar. The admin user is already added by default and assigned a System Administrator role. To view the user associated with this organization, click the Users tab from the current organization.

When creating users, you have three roles to assign to the user which include Normal User, System Auditor, and System Administrator, all of which have different access available to them. You also create teams that you can assign users to, and when you create a new project to work with, you will then assign these projects to a team. If the user is not part of the team, they will not be able to access the project. Of course, the installation comes with a default team that all users and projects can be assigned to until you create your own.

Figure 9-4 shows the form presented when you create a new user in AWX Ansible Tower. As you can see, it is intuitive and self-explanatory.

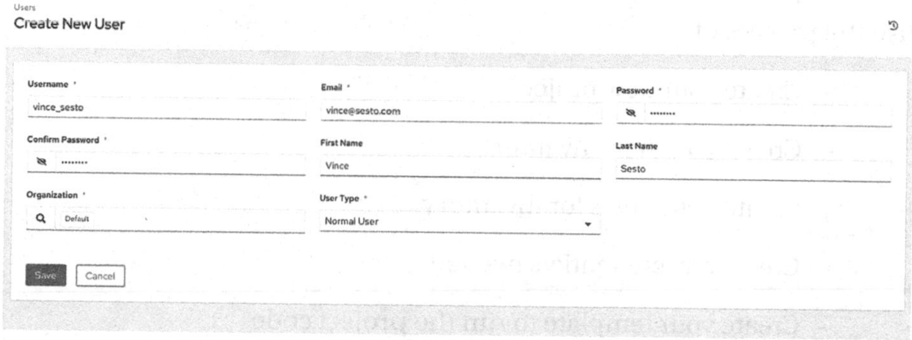

Figure 9-4. The Form Presented When Creating New Users

User access and management is one of the main benefits that AWX Ansible Tower provides as it allows you to not have to consider all these aspects when setting up how your team can access your configuration management code. As we mentioned earlier, the settings menu also allows you to use your corporate access management like Active Directory instead of needing to specify users and access.

An alternative option could be to allow different access via your code repository, as this is a similar way in which you could assign access to specific teams instead of allowing all your users to have access to all your Ansible code.

Introducing Projects

Within AWX Ansible Tower, we use Projects to manage our work whether it be a role or playbook that performs our configuration management. You create a project and add in your code, whether it be a code repository or a file or directory. You then create a template to run your code, specifying the playbook that should be automatically found, and this template will then run against your hosts file. To create a new project from start to finish, I use the process of

- Create your new project

- Create your new inventory

- Create your hosts for inventory

- Create any credentials needed

- Create your template to run the project code

In the following section, we will walk you through setting up a test project to work on AWX Ansible Tower.

Note   The example that we are working through in the following section is the same code that we used in the last chapter as part of our Molecule testing and can be located at the following GitHub link: https://github.com/vincesesto/test_role.

Setting Up a Project

If you click the Projects option under the Resources section, you should see the "Demo Project" provided as part of your installation. By either clicking the link for the project or clicking the Edit icon to the right of the screen, it will allow you to review or make changes to the Project.

To create your own project, you click the Add button. As you can see in Figure 9-5, setting up your project is pretty clear, making sure you add your project name, in our example "Test Role" and description. You need to link the project to your code; in our instance, we have added the GitHub location of the code, in case you need to add credentials for a private repository. If you have your code in a file or directory, you will need to import it onto the AWX Ansible Tower server in the /var/lib/awx/projects directory location.

Projects
Create New Project

Name *	Description	Organization *
Test Role	This is a test role to test our project	Q Default

Source Control Credential Type *

Git

Type Details

Source Control URL * ⓧ	Source Control Branch/Tag/Commit ⓧ	Source Control Refspec ⓧ
https://github.com/vincesesto/test_role	main	

Source Control Credential

Q

Options

☑ Clean ⓧ   ☐ Delete ⓧ   ☐ Update Revision on Launch ⓧ   ☐ Allow Branch Override ⓧ

Figure 9-5. *The Form Presented When Creating New Project*

Once you save your new project, you will then need to create hosts to deploy the project on and a template.

Inventories and Hosts

So far, when working in Ansible, we have been using the terms inventory and hosts interchangeably. In AWX Ansible Tower, an inventory is more like a lable or container, which then includes one or more hosts files. A good example of this is similar to the way we can create a directory to hold a number of hosts files. The name of the directory will be the inventory.

You will need to create an inventory before you create your hosts files, because when you create your hosts, you need to add them to a specific inventory at the time of creation. Each of the options for inventory and hosts should be clear from this point. Of course, select Hosts from the Resources menu and click Add to create your new hosts.

Figure 9-6 shows an example of our test project that we have now created, "test hosts," and assigned to the inventory of "Test Inventory." We have specified the local host in the variables section available.

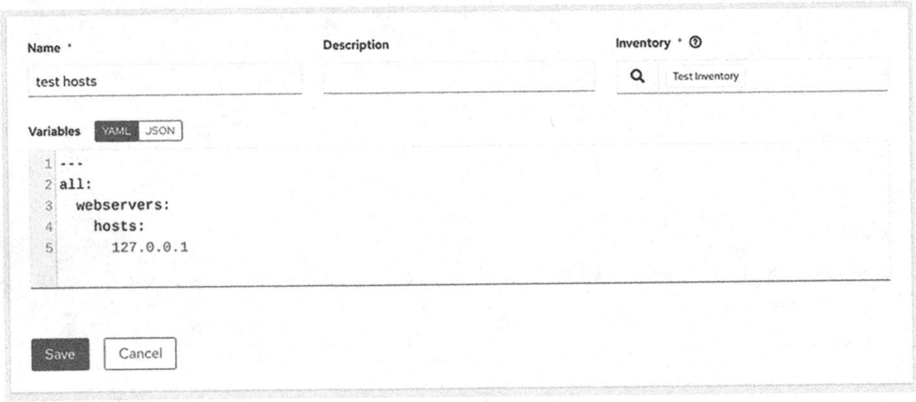

Figure 9-6. *Creating New Hosts in AWX Ansible Tower*

By creating your hosts and project, this should now give you enough information to allow you to create a template to run your Ansible code.

Note   AWX Ansible Tower also allows you to create both Credentials and Variables as part of your projects. As we have been doing this within our code, there is no real need to do this in AWX, but please note that the option is available.

Creating Templates for a Project

Once you have your project, inventories, and hosts set up, you can now start to look at your template to run your project. When you click the Templates option under the Resources section of the menu, you will see there is the Demo Template available as part of AWX installation, which will run as part of the Demo Project. To create your own template, click the Add button, which will take you to a form similar to the one in the following.

As you can see, once you link this template to a project, it will then be able to provide you with a list of playbooks available in the code. You will need to make sure if it has a valid playbook to run and also provide it with an inventory of hosts to run this code on. With the example provided, you will notice that it will detect any playbook including the tests directory and tasks available in the repository. Our following example has used a simple playbook called deploy_on_awx.yml that simply provides prints "Deploy from AWX Ansible Tower" in the Ansible output.

The template form also gives you the option to create a schedule to have this playbook run on a specific date or even daily or weekly. Once the template is created, even if you have not set up a schedule, you are able to then run the job whenever you like via the web interface.

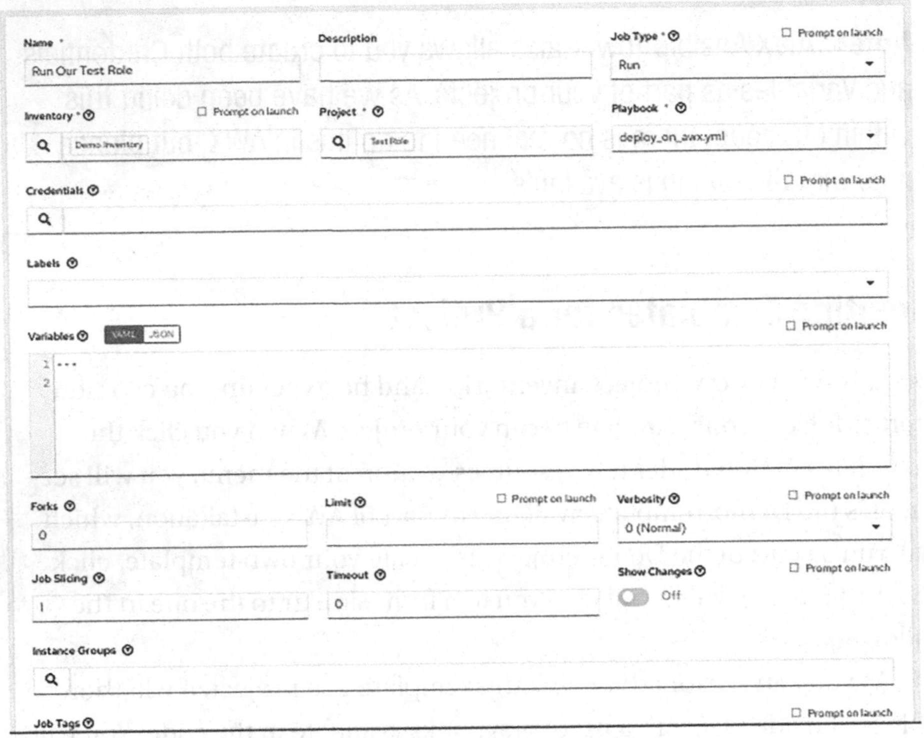

Figure 9-7. *Creating New Template in AWX Ansible Tower*

Running Your Job for a Project

Actually, running your job can be done in a number of different ways you can use the template of your project and click the Launch button in the interface. You can use the Jobs option from the Views menu. It will give you a list of all the jobs available. From the Jobs menu, the Launch button is shaped like a small rocket, and this will run your job for you as well. Figure 9-8 provides you with an example of how the interface looks.

| | | 8 – Run Our Test Role | Playbook Run | 05/06/2022, 16:51:49 | |
| | | 7 – Demo Project | Source Control Update | 05/06/2022, 16:47:30 | |

Figure 9-8. *Running Your Project Job*

By clicking on any of the jobs listed, we get a detailed breakdown of the job including timings and extra details of the job. By clicking the Output tab, we also see the Ansible output as we have become used to on the command line, detailing how the Ansible task was run.

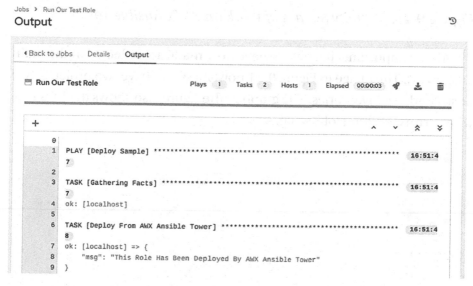

Figure 9-9. *Display the Ansible Output of Your Job*

AWX Ansible Tower keeps a record of all the work performed in the Activity Stream. This includes any work such as creating users to editing projects. Now that we have set up our new project, we can see the work that has been performed by clicking the Activity Stream option under views. An example is shown in Figure 9-10 of what the activity stream looks like, and clicking into each item will give you further information of each.

Activity Stream

Dashboard (all activity) ▾

Keyword ▾			🔍	1 - 20 of 47 ▾ ‹ ›
Time ↓	**Initiated by**	**Event**		**Actions**
05/06/2022, 16:34:39	admin	created project Test Role		🔍
05/06/2022, 16:26:24	admin	associated Default member_role to vince_sesto		🔍
05/06/2022, 16:26:24	admin	updated user vince_sesto		🔍

Figure 9-10. *Activity Stream of Work on AWX Ansible Tower*

All the important changes we have now made are reflected in the main dashboard. The image in Figure 9-11 now shows we have two projects, two hosts, and two inventories. The graph in the figure also shows the jobs run, with no unsuccessful jobs so far.

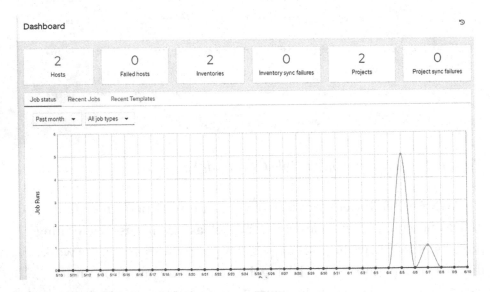

Figure 9-11. *Our Dashboard After Work Performed*

In this part of the chapter, we have only given you a quick run through of using AWX. Although we have not spent too much time, the knowledge of Ansible that you currently have should allow you to work with the intuitive interface that AWX provides. I honestly feel you don't need Ansible Tower or AWX to properly manage your environment, and I have seen a lot of people use Ansible on large environments without using Ansible Tower to manage their environment.

I do see AWX and Ansible Tower to be a nice extension of Ansible. It allows you to manage who has access to your configuration management as well as schedule jobs and deployments with a nice user interface that keeps a record of jobs and deployments.

Summary

You have now reached the end of this chapter where we have tried to help you look at possibly ways you can implement your Ansible code in larger server environments. We started by looking at your host and inventory files and worked through some of the extra functionality that we had not previously covered to help you manage the servers you are working with. We also had a look at using inventory plugins for dynamic hosts that are constantly changing.

The second half of this chapter looked at using Ansible Tower, specifically the open source version AWX, which we installed onto our working system and showed you some of the basic concepts and features and discussed how you can use your own Ansible playbooks within Ansible Tower.

The end of this chapter also brings us to the end of this book. Throughout this book, we have covered a lot of ground. We introduced configuration management and discussed why we choose Ansible to do the work for automating our configuration management. We introduced Ansible modules and gave your details on how to use them and then how to turn them into function Ansible playbooks.

We then took our playbooks further and turned them into roles and started using more powerful features of Ansible like templates, Ansible Vault, and Ansible Galaxy and showed you how you can start to make your own modules for your custom work. We then took our work into the Amazon Cloud and showed you how to implement your configuration management into fully functioning servers using different AWS services.

The last parts of the book focused on troubleshooting potential issues with your work as well as testing your code before you make any changes, before commencing this chapter.

Index

A

Printed in the United States
by Baker & Taylor Publisher Services